THE EDUCATION ACT
1870

THE EDUCATION ACT, 1870

Text and Commentary

James Murphy

Reader in Education, University of Liverpool

David & Charles . Newton Abbot

For
P. M. K. M.

ISBN 0 7153 5438 8

Set in ten on twelve point Baskerville
and printed in Great Britain
by W. J. Holman Limited Dawlish
for David & Charles (Publishers) Limited
South Devon House   Newton Abbot   Devon

CONTENTS

SECTION ONE

THE
HISTORICAL BACKGROUND

[Note: throughout this book the references in parentheses are to sections of the Act (s), and to Hansard, *Parliamentary Debates,* Third Series (H)]

1 The Climate of Political and Economic Theory

The Elementary Education Act of 1870 did not inaugurate in Britain the provision of state aid for public elementary schools: such aid had been furnished on a growing scale for almost forty years. Nor did it introduce a national system wholly maintained from public funds. It was not even intended to apply to the whole of the United Kingdom, since Scotland and Ireland were expressly excluded from its provisions (s 2). It did, however, decree that henceforward there must be made available throughout England and Wales 'a sufficient amount of accommodation in public elementary schools' (s 5); and it recognised that this would entail financial support from both national and local taxes. Though the state declined to accept full responsibility for providing a national system of elementary education, it did, at least, undertake to ensure that such a system would be established.

But the action was extremely belated. Not to speak of earlier suggestions, at intervals over more than two generations (beginning with Samuel Whitbread's Bill of 1807) individuals and governments had proposed the use of public money to promote the nation-wide provision of elementary education; and for at least forty years governments had been repeatedly reminded that 'the great defect of English education . . . is the want of a national organisation . . . It forms the one great exception to the civilised world'.[1] One cannot fully comprehend or account for the merits and deficiencies of the Act of 1870 unless the forces which caused this long delay are understood.

Some of these factors can be indicated briefly, though this should not suggest that they were unimportant. In the early years of the century there had been fears that an educated populace might turn to subversion, refuse to obey superiors, or desert their menial tasks; but apprehension of this kind had been considerably allayed by the evidence drawn from other countries, and it was often countered by the assertion that more extensive education would lead to improvement of conduct and a diminution in crime. Again, it was argued that state intervention in the field of education might lead to tyranny and repression; and the doctrine of laissez faire was adduced in the endeavour to demonstrate how useless, or even harmful, government interference might be. Such contentions were frequently rebutted by reference to the great importance attached to popular education by the very political theorists quoted: it was even maintained that educated workmen, being able to understand the economic doctrines then current, would appreciate the futility of agitating for better pay and conditions.

Nevertheless four principles emerged from the rather confused general climate of opinion concerning political and economic theory which had its origins in somewhat crude versions of the teachings of Adam Smith, Jeremy Bentham and their followers. These were:

(i) That state intervention to supply and finance education would endanger freedom of thought.

(ii) That such intervention, since it would cause a decline in competition and reduce personal initiative and incentive, would lead to inefficiency and waste, if there were not close inspection and control.

(iii) That government aid, if given at all, must so operate as not to discourage voluntary charitable activity but to stimulate it.

(iv) That parents, in particular, must be expected to make some payment, however small, towards the cost of educating their children; otherwise they would be failing in their duty, would become feckless, and would not appreciate the value of education.

Naturally, the insistence on the importance of voluntary contributions and on the payment of school fees was welcomed by governments indisposed to spend large sums on elementary education; but it is important to note that in fact nearly all of those most genuinely anxious to promote the education of the poor accepted these principles without question[2], at least until the years immediately preceding 1870. It will be made clear later how such ideas operated to delay the establishment of a national system of elementary education, and to restrict the amount and quality of such instruction that could be made available.

2 The Religious Problem

But undoubtedly the greatest hindrance to the comprehensive

provision of elementary education arose from differences of religious belief.

In earlier centuries many factors had led to the supervision, and often the supply, of education coming to be regarded as the peculiar province of the church: among these were the close relationship between church and state; the importance of religion in the spiritual and social life of the nation; the conviction that religion must be a fundamental part of all education; the church's widespread organisation and great financial resources; the philanthropy of religious believers and the parsimony of governments; the constant need to train priests and other servants of the church; the importance attached within and without the church to the teaching of Latin; the free time available to many of the clergy; and so on.

By the middle of the nineteenth century some of these factors had disappeared or become much less important. Perhaps the most significant developments had been the weakening of the links between the Church of England and the state, the divisions among religious believers (caused particularly by the rise of Nonconformity), the great decline in the influence of religious organisations on the poorer classes, and the vastly increased need for secular instruction in a modern industrialised society. In 1870 it was still very generally agreed that religious instruction was a valuable, even necessary, part of the instruction of young children; but what form this should take, and, indeed, whether it should be given at all in schools assisted by the state (instead of being left to parents and churches), were matters hotly disputed. The attitudes of the parties chiefly concerned must therefore be considered.[3]

As is well known, the rise of the Sunday-school movement had affected all the denominations in the last decades of the eighteenth century, and subsequently the adoption of the inexpensive monitorial system had led to the establishment of many elementary schools by individual churches, chapels and private donors. In order to co-ordinate the efforts made on behalf of the Church of England schools, to collect funds, and otherwise to assist the movement, the church set up in 1811 an association which described itself unequivocally as 'The National Society for Promoting the Education of the Poor in the Principles of the Church of England'. Its rules were equally clear: though children of all sects might be admitted to schools affiliated to it, all pupils must read the Authorised Version of the Bible, must be taught the church liturgy and catechism, and must attend an Anglican church on Sundays; whilst all teachers must be members of the Church of England.

As the 'Established Church of the Realm', whose head was the head of the state, the Church of England felt entitled to claim, and was accorded, a superior status. Among other privileges, its bishops sat in the House of Lords; it could call upon even those outside its communion to contribute to any church rate levied for the repair of the nave of the parish church and the upkeep of the churchyard; and only professed Anglicans were admitted to Oxford University or awarded degrees at Cambridge. Until about 1840 (and more rarely later) the claim was even sometimes made that the Established Church had the sole right to supply and supervise the elementary education of the people of Britain. Such privileges and claims became more and more unreal as the political influence of other religious bodies increased during the century, and they were naturally resented by many members of these other sects. A great deal of the bitterness to which discussions on educational provision often gave rise sprang from the underlying hostility, suspicion, even scorn for each other's professional claims, among clergy of the different denominations.

Another society resembling in its organisation the National Society had been founded (in its original form) in 1808 to encourage the spread of elementary education; but the proclaimed purpose of this 'British and Foreign School Society' was to promote 'the Education of the Labouring and Manufacturing Classes of Society of every Religious Persuasion'. Though the 'lessons for reading' would be 'extracts from the Holy Scriptures' (in the Authorised Version), 'no catechism or peculiar religious tenets' would be taught in the schools, and each child would be 'enjoined to attend regularly the place of worship to which its parents belong'. The society was widely supported, mainly by Nonconformists, but also by others who deplored the more exclusive policy of the National Society; nevertheless, since teachers in schools connected with the British Society were allowed to give explanations of the biblical passages read (according to 'the plain and obvious meaning of the text'),[4] and since the instruction given was decidedly Evangelical,[5] the teaching was regarded by many as being not, in fact, 'unsectarian'. Objections were raised by Unitarians; and the Roman Catholic clergy, though often willing in the early decades of the century to allow children of their faith to attend schools established by other denominations (provided that no religious proselytism was attempted), refused to sanction the reading of the Authorised Version of the Bible.

When, in 1833, the government made its first small grant of £20,000 to encourage the development of elementary education, it evaded many difficulties by allowing the National and the British societies to act, so to speak, as its agents. The government needed to make no controversial demand for continuing inspection and control of the schools assisted, since the grants were once-for-all payments towards building costs: the state reserved the right to call for 'periodical reports' from school managers, but none was ever asked for. The condition was laid down that at least half of the building cost must come from voluntary contributions; this requirement was in accordance with the contemporary economic 'conventional wisdom' mentioned earlier, and, moreover, since it favoured the Church of England (with its greater financial resources), it disarmed to some extent the objection that equal recognition had been given to the largely Nonconformist British Society. Again, much bitter controversy was avoided by the decision that there could be no question of granting aid for Roman Catholic schools or for Nonconformist denominational schools, such as those of the Wesleyans.

Unfortunately for the state, however, difficulties would not disappear simply because they were ignored. There were three main obstacles to continued peace:

(i) Small parliamentary grants were quite inadequate, since voluntary contributions could not, even with them, provide and maintain schools on the scale urgently required; whilst increased state assistance, on the other hand, must surely lead ultimately to increased government involvement, supervision, even control.

(ii) The political emancipation of the Nonconformists and Roman Catholics in 1828-9 and the passing of the Reform Bill in 1832 were merely the latest acknowledgements of the fact that something approaching equal treatment for all religious groups could not permanently be denied.

(iii) There emerged in remarkably different quarters a

growing conviction that the state must not concern itself with the teaching of religion. This raised particular problems, since it often went with an equally strong conviction that religious instruction must be an integral and inseparable part of all elementary education. Sometimes, as we shall see, the opposition to state intervention in this sphere arose from philosophic or theological considerations (or from political opposition disguised as such), sometimes merely from the reluctance to pay taxes for the propagation of religious views considered to be false.

Faced with the need to encourage the development of a national system of education, whilst treating all denominations alike and avoiding any interference with religious instruction, the state had several courses open to it.

It might have undertaken to provide or subsidise only secular education, leaving religious instruction to be given (where desired) outside the schools, or at least outside normal school hours, by parents, clergymen or others. This policy was constantly advocated as the only practicable solution to the problem by many (including great numbers of Nonconformists) who had strong religious convictions, and, of course, by some, also, who had no religious convictions at all. It was, however, quite unacceptable to those who maintained that religious and secular instruction must on no account be separated, and that a religious 'atmosphere' must infuse the whole work of the school.

Again, the state might have set up or assisted schools in which only 'non-sectarian' religion was taught; but many sincerely believed that there could be no such religious teaching, or that it would lead to cynicism and scepticism, or that it would not fulfil the aims of the various religious groups whose support was required.

Some difficulties might have been obviated if the state had agreed to provide separate denominational schools for the various sects—but this was considered quite impracticable. since it would not only have alienated those opposed to state support for religious instruction (especially instruction in a religion believed to be harmfully erroneous), but would often have entailed the quite uneconomic establishment of a number of schools, each attended by very small groups of children, in districts where one school would well suffice ('single-school areas').

So far, the state has been referred to as if it was a monolithic entity seeking in a rational and uncommitted way to solve an organisational problem. But of course governments included representatives of the various disputing groups, and, quite apart from divergent attitudes inspired by sincerely held beliefs, the two-party system encouraged the view that it was the duty of parliamentary oppositions to oppose. In general the Conservative party favoured, and looked for support from, the members of the Church of England, whilst the Liberals had similar links with the Nonconformists; the small but influential group of Radicals were generally in agreement with those Nonconformists who favoured government support for secular instruction only, or, if that was impracticable, for only such religious instruction in addition as could be described as unsectarian.

3 The Rejected Initiatives of 1839-43

Between 1839 and 1843 the pattern of future conflicts was made clear. In the former year the Liberals attempted to take the first tentative step towards founding a state-provided system of education when Lord John Russell, as Home Secretary, proposed the establishment of a single teacher-training college (with a model school attached) to admit members of all sects, who would receive denominational instruction from their various clergymen. To circumvent the charge that secular and religious instruction would thus be separated, Russell proposed that all the students would also be given unsectarian religious instruction together, as part of the normal daily routine. (This attempt to deal with the 'religious problem' was based on arrangements which had recently proved reasonably acceptable in Ireland[6] and in the two Corporation Schools in Liverpool[7]).

There was also provision for setting up a committee of the Privy Council (to be known as the Committee of Council on Education) 'to superintend the application of any sums voted by parliament for the purpose of promoting Education'. The government had tried to acknowledge suitably the special status of the Church of England by arranging for the official (salaried) chaplain to be an Anglican, but this merely angered members of other churches whilst failing to prevent a storm of vigorous and bitter opposition from many Conservatives and Anglicans. The proposal to establish the training college was quickly withdrawn, but the Committee of Council remained precariously in existence, its survival ensured by a Commons majority of only two.

In 1843 it was the turn of the Conservatives to try their hand: Sir James Graham's Factory Bill of that year contained proposals for the education of children living in workhouses or employed in a very limited number of factories, the schools to be built with government loans and maintained from local poor-rates. The suggested regulations would have ensured that the schoolmaster and the religious instruction given would have been Anglican; the local Anglican clergyman would have been one of the managers and in most places the majority of these would also have been members of the Established Church. The Nonconformists strenuously objected, being not in the least placated by the provision that children might be withdrawn from religious instruction on grounds of conscience. Even when concessions were made permitting, inter alia, a more equitable system for electing managers and the provision of religious instruction once a week by licensed Nonconformist ministers, strong opposition continued, and the controversial proposals relating to education had to be withdrawn.

4 The Conflict Intensified

Both of the great political parties had thus endeavoured to deal with the religious problem, and their efforts had not only ignominiously failed but had aroused such vehement anger that both were for decades extremely reluctant to try again.

Their failure had other very important results. The Roman Catholics became convinced that, though they had relatively few schools of their own, and no strong middle class to give financial support, they must depend on their own efforts to provide schools: within a very short time they had adopted the position that only fully denominational Roman Catholic schools could meet the needs of Roman Catholic children. There could be no compromise, no restriction as to the amount or kind of religious instruction given, no agreement to confine such instruction to limited times, no sharing of premises with other denominations, since all these would prevent the creation of a wholly Roman Catholic 'atmosphere'.

The Nonconformist attitude similarly hardened. The Wesleyans, who normally felt no strong hostility to the Church of England, had made great efforts to provide their own schools and were inclined to stand aside from the conflict; however, they were particularly anxious that whatever steps the state might take to promote education should not encourage the dissemination of Roman Catholic doctrines, and on this ground they had supported the Established Church in its denunciation of the Liberal government's proposals of 1839.

But members of some other Nonconformist groups now became much more militant. It had from the beginning been a fundamental part of their beliefs that the state must not concern itself with religion; and, of course, their adherence to this principle was strengthened by resentment of the privileges and special status accorded to the despised 'state church', for whose support, as has been pointed out, they could be obliged to pay 'church rates'. Since religious instruction was so widely considered to be an essential and integral part of education, it seemed clear to many of them that state control of, or even assistance to, education, must involve intervention in religious affairs outside the proper jurisdiction of the state.

The conscientious scruples of many Nonconformists could be satisfied, however, if it could be shown that no part of any state grant was spent on religious instruction: thus some felt that religious instruction ought to be given outside normal school hours, whilst many had found it possible to support the British Society by postulating that a single initial grant in aid of building did not constitute state support for religious teaching given after the school was built. The willingness recently shown by the state to recognise the political rights of Nonconformists had somewhat allayed the suspicions and hostility of many of them.

But the educational proposals of both the Liberal and Conservative governments had included some acknowledgement of the primacy of the Established Church; the ensuing controversies, and the successful opposition to the educational clauses of the Factory Bill of 1843, had not only aroused animosity but had

B

demonstrated to the more active Nonconformists what political power they now possessed. Especially among many Congregationalists and Baptists, even the small state grant already made available in aid of school building came under attack, particularly as theological convictions about the proper role of the state were fortified when (because of the requirement concerning voluntary contributions) most of the grant was seen to be spent on schools dedicated to 'Promoting the Education of the Poor in the Principles of the Church of England'.

A 'Voluntaryist' movement arose from 1843, led by Edward Baines, a Congregationalist and editor of the *Leeds Mercury*, and Edward Miall, a Radical and a Congregational minister, editor of *The Nonconformist*. The policy of the Voluntaryists was simply and vigorously expressed: they objected to all state support for education as involving a threat to political liberty, personal initiative and parental responsibility; as being a departure from sound economic theory; and, above all, as constituting not only state interference in the sphere of religion but a violation of the consciences of those forced to pay taxes in support of religious doctrines they considered false and pernicious. Accepting the logic of their position, the Voluntaryists collected funds and encouraged voluntary efforts to promote education. By 1851 they had built 364 schools and a training college, without any state assistance.

The Church of England, too, had become increasingly vigorous, partly because of the need to defend its position, but even more because of the rise of the Tractarian (Oxford) movement from 1833. The new emphasis on the divine mission of the church and of its clergy did much to inspire in both an increased sense of purpose; but the movement gave rise also to divisions and dissension within, and to much hostility from without. The leadership, of course, came from such men as Newman, Keble and Manning, but in the sphere of education its most forceful spokesman was the Rev G. A. Denison, who tirelessly made clear what, in his view, the new teachings entailed. In particular, he claimed that religious instruction could never be unsectarian and must be an integral part of education; that educational provision must therefore lie wholly within the province of the church and outside that of the state; but that it was the duty of the state, nevertheless, to furnish financial and material support as required, it being understood that this must not give rise to claims for inspection and control.

Such demands, of course, alienated the Nonconformists, confirmed their worst fears, and stiffened their opposition to any state system of education which would have brought public elementary schools under the influence of Church of England clergymen. Moreover, not only Nonconformists but many Anglicans were made openly hostile by what was commonly described as the 'Romanising' tendencies of the new movement; the Wesleyans, hitherto, as we have seen, of all Nonconformists the most sympathetic to the Established Church, were particularly shocked at the admiration evinced for Roman Catholic practices, and were further antagonised since the new insistence on the apostolic succession of the priesthood reinforced existing Anglican unwillingness to accept the credentials of Wesleyan ministers.

5 The Committee of Council and the Churches

Meanwhile, in the midst of all this turbulence, the Committee of Council on Education most surprisingly continued to exist; and it did so because for both political parties it represented the only vehicle for continued state encouragement of elementary education. Its president was the Lord President of the Council (since he, as such, was president of all Privy Council committees); the other members were also members of the government of the day, and they included the Home Secretary and the Chancellor of the Exchequer. However, the practical administration was largely in the hands of the non-political permanent secretary. Its regulations and reports were laid before parliament annually and were acted upon if not successfully opposed: this obviated the need to introduce legislation and made possible quiet, piecemeal progress without encouraging dramatic confrontations on wide issues of policy.

The first secretary to the Committee of Council was Dr James Phillips Kay, who adopted the name Kay-Shuttleworth in 1842. He was a very able administrator and was quite determined that 'the feuds of sects and the interests of bodies incompetent effectually to deal with this national question should not rob the people of a national system of education'.[8] The vehement controversies of 1839 and 1843 convinced him that the state could not hope to take the provision of elementary education out of the hands of the separate religious communions; but since these, equally obviously, would need increased financial support and expert advice, governments might well expect to be allowed some supervision and control of secular education. The Voluntaryists asked for no state aid, and therefore no problem arose with them; but the committee of the National Society included many Tractarians and others who considered state interference with church schools to be quite unacceptable—not altogether unreasonably, if continuing government intervention were to be the price of the single state contribution towards building costs.

In 1839 the Committee of Council proposed that no further grant should be made 'unless the right of inspection be retained, in order to secure a conformity to the regulations and discipline established in the several schools, with such improvements as may from time to time be suggested by the Committee'.[9] But the newly-created Committee had overplayed its hand and had nothing like the political support necessary to win the day: when the National Society angrily protested, and the government grants already offered for many schools were firmly rejected, the Committee was compelled to adopt a much more accommodating tone. It had to agree that inspectors, far from exercising control, must merely offer advice and information, and even these only when they were asked for. The Committee formally stated that it was 'strongly of the opinion that no plan of education ought to be encouraged in which intellectual instruction is not subordinate to the regulation of the thoughts and habits of the children by the doctrines and precepts of revealed religion'.[10] This, of course, ruled out grants for schools giving only secular instruction.

The terms which the Church of England insisted upon in relation to its own schools included these:

(i) Since secular and religious instruction must be regarded as indivisible, government inspectors must deal with both.

(ii) The appropriate archbishop must be consulted before inspectors were appointed: these must be Anglicans (the first inspectors were in fact clergymen), and the archbishops could not only propose suitable candidates but ensure the dismissal of an inspector subsequently considered unsatisfactory.

(iii) The archbishops would issue the directives relating to the inspection of religious teaching and also have the right to examine the more general instructions to inspectors (that is, those concerning the inspection of secular education), before they were sanctioned by the Committee of Council.

(iv) Copies of an inspector's report on a school must be sent to the appropriate bishop and archbishop.

The agreement thus accepted by the Committee in 1840 was henceforward commonly referred to as the 'Concordat': it was still in force, as we shall see, in 1870.

It will be convenient here to note that, after some hesitation, the Committee of Council accorded to the British Society in 1843 the right to be consulted about an inspector's appointment; when grants became payable in respect of Wesleyan and Roman Catholic schools from 1847 this right was again conceded, but not the power possessed by the Anglicans to propose suitable inspectors or to ensure the dismissal of unsatisfactory ones. Moreover the bodies who respectively controlled the British, Wesleyan and Roman Catholic schools declined on principle to permit government inspection of religious instruction.

6 Increasing State Influence

The Committee of Council had thus felt obliged to bow to the wishes of the Church of England leaders, but at least a system of state inspection had been established; and various factors soon combined to strengthen the Committee's position in relation to the church. The sweeping claims made by the Tractarians as to the proper role and status of the clergy, whilst naturally gratifying to some clerics, made others uneasy as smacking of 'Popery', and they alienated many laymen. The demand for state aid without state supervision and control flew in the face of accepted opinion; moreover, as state support had continually to be increased, this demand became ever more difficult to justify among those holding less extreme views.

In 1846, at the instigation of Kay-Shuttleworth, the Committee of Council inaugurated a system of teacher-training by which suitable pupils were apprenticed to schoolmasters and might eventually win scholarships enabling them to attend training colleges. Since state grants were consequently made to the pupils, to the schoolmasters and to the college authorities, and as payments were made also to augment the salaries of teachers who qualified, the scheme involved a relatively vast increase in government expenditure on elementary education, especially as its purpose was to increase greatly the number of teachers employed and get rid of the cheap but inefficient monitorial system.

One obvious result was to make increased government supervision seem inevitable, for, whatever theories might be held concerning the respective roles of church and state, schoolmasters would have to be approved as fit to train pupils, and the latter must be repeatedly examined—before, during, and at the end of their period in a training college—since annual grants would depend upon the progress made. Inspectors could no longer be mere advisers. Further, the greatly increased provision now made from public funds made the exclusion of any from its benefits on religious grounds the more unjust: hence the necessary extension of aid to the Wesleyan and Roman Catholic authorities just noted.

But two other problems were less easily solved. First: how were such benefits to be made available to the children of minority groups in single-school areas? The Committee of Council wished to have written into the trust deeds of schools receiving state aid a 'conscience clause', that is, a formal declaration that children might be withdrawn from religious instruction and excused attendance at church on Sundays if their parents so requested on conscientious grounds. The Wesleyans already acted upon this principle, and the rules of the British Society formally required that religious instruction should not be sectarian. The Roman Catholics were reluctant to accept a conscience clause, since to do so might imply recognition of a separation between religious and secular instruction, but they agreed to permit withdrawal from denominational instruction,[11] being no doubt influenced to some extent by the considerations that there were relatively few areas in which the only school was Roman Catholic, and that Protestant parents were commonly unwilling to send their children to Roman Catholic schools.

But the official attitude of the National Society was much more rigid. In practice Anglican clergymen not infrequently excused children of other sects from attendance for religious instruction and worship, especially when the schools concerned received government grants.[12] The Committee of the National Society, however, largely under the influence of the Tractarians, maintained that the regulations of the society forbade any compromise on this point.[13] It was claimed that the prime purpose of the National Society, and of the schools affiliated to it, must be to teach the doctrines of the Church of England; that religious and secular instruction must not be separated; and that, even if the rules might be relaxed, the state must not demand this as of right, in return for financial help. So intense was the opposition that it was not until 1860 that the state nerved itself to demand the insertion of a conscience clause in the trust deeds of any new school for which a building grant was made and which would become the single school in its area. Since existing schools were not affected and the National Society did not officially accept the ruling, the problem remained acute.

A second issue which had direct relevance to the Act of 1870, and which was important because of its implications, was the subject of lay control of secular education in state-aided church schools. There was never any question that the control and supervision of religious instruction must remain the province of the clergy; but as assistance from public funds increased, and since a great deal of the financial support involved came from laymen (including parents), it could be argued that secular instruction should be controlled by lay managers. Kay-Shuttleworth was particularly anxious to ensure this. The Wesleyans had already accepted the principle; the Roman Catholics did so with some reluctance; the rules of the National Society did not preclude such an arrangement; but once again, state interference was deeply resented by those Anglicans who sought to emphasise the exalted mission of the Church of England.

A crucial point was: who should decide, the clerical or the lay managers, whether a disputed topic fell within the range of religious or of secular instruction? Here, the Roman Catholics were adamant: accustomed to lay subordination to the clergy, they would brook no interference from lay opinion, still less government intervention, in such a case. But the claims of the more extreme of the Anglican clergy were regarded with some suspicion by many of the laity, and even by many of their clerical colleagues, especially after Newman, the most influential of the Tractarians, went over to the Roman Catholic church in 1845. The Committee of Council was, therefore, able to insist (1848), in relation to disputes about spheres of control, that the grant of aid to new Church of England schools would be conditional on acceptance of provision for an arbitration procedure allowing in principle not only for lay, but for some degree of state, representation.

These disputes divided and weakened the Church of England and strengthened the position of the Committee of Council. They led many of those anxious to see the establishment of a national system of elementary education to feel (whatever their own views on religion might be) that no such system could be created until education was taken out of the hands of clergymen and was confined to secular instruction.

7 The Newcastle Commission

Since such controversy and animosity had been inspired even by the state's unambitious policy of confining its efforts to the support and partial control of schools established by the various religious bodies, it is not surprising that most political leaders fought shy of proposing any more comprehensive plan involving complete government responsibility for the supply and maintenance of a national system. Moreover, by the middle of the century governments were becoming uneasy about the expenditure on education to which they already found themselves committed. In 1853, twenty years after the initial parliamentary grant of £20,000 had been made, the state's contribution to the cost of building schools and training colleges, of training teachers, supplementing salaries and providing equipment, together with the charges involved in maintaining an inspectorate and a central administrative machinery, amounted to well over £250,000.[14] From that year, being anxious to ensure that more use was made of the schools provided, the state began paying capitation grants based upon numbers of children who attended with reasonable regularity. Even though the usual stipulation was made as to financial support being forthcoming from voluntary contributors and parents, by 1859 the annual government grant had risen to more than £723,000.[15]

The government set up in 1858 a royal commission under the Duke of Newcastle to 'inquire into the state of popular education in England, and to consider and report what measures, if any, were required for the extension of sound and cheap elementary instruction to all classes of the people'. In its report (1861) the commission praised the absence of government control over the direct management of schools and, indeed, recommended that, in future, state grants in respect of teachers and pupil teachers should be made not to the individuals concerned but to the school managers, who would decide upon the salaries to be paid. A further proposal was that financial support for schools should come not only from state taxes but from county or borough rates; this rate aid would be administered by local education boards, amounts granted to depend on the results of examining individual children in the three R's.

A little earlier (1856) the state had recognised the constantly growing importance of the Committee of Council by giving it a more direct link with parliament: henceforward it was to have a responsible parliamentary 'head of department', who would rank as vice-president of the Council and be a member of the government of the day. The detailed administrative duties nominally supervised by the somewhat remote Commitee of Council would be attended to by an Education Department. Robert Lowe, vice-president of the Council, formulated a Revised Code (1862) consolidating the regulations relating to state-aided schools, and he took the opportunity to include provisions based on those recommendations of the Newcastle Commission of which the government approved. A new system of 'payment by results' was introduced; this was not to apply to children under six, and even for older children part of the grant payable would be based on meeting requirements as to satisfactory attendance, but schools would be very largely dependent for their income (and teachers for the salaries they could obtain from school managers) on the individual examination results.

Two points about the new arrangements are particularly worth noting in view of later events. Firstly, that state grants toward the cost of building training colleges were discontinued, so that those religious groups already well provided with colleges now had a distinct advantage over others. Secondly, since 'payment by results' was initially related to success in the three R's, it seemed likely that teachers and managers would henceforth be inclined to attach less importance to religious instruction. Here the Church of England was in a privileged position. As we have seen, unlike the other bodies concerned, it had from the first insisted that such instruction should fall within the province of government inspectors, and it now successfully claimed that the 'Concordat' of 1840 must continue to operate. The Committee of Council accepted the proposition that, in Anglican schools alone, any grant 'earned' by results would be wholly or partially withheld if the inspector considered the religious instruction unsatisfactory.[16]

The Newcastle Commission's recommendation that government grants could be supplemented from local rates was not accepted by the state, in spite of its strong desire to reduce the amount derived from taxes. There were three main difficulties:

(1) Outside the larger towns there was usually no adequate system of local government: such bodies as did exist were normally under the influence of local landowners and were therefore not well regarded by those who were not Conservative in politics and Anglican in religion.

(ii) Local financial support for education would involve some degree of local control, and this was feared, both on general grounds by those who opposed government intervention in religious affairs, and also because, in different parts of the country, the prevailing religious opinions among those in authority might prevent fair treatment of one or more religious groups.

(iii) Existing conscientious objections to government support for religious instruction (especially when this was considered false) would be particularly stimulated if funds were not drawn from general taxation but were provided by a rate levied for a specific and recognisable educational purpose.

8 Parliamentary Deadlock

The bitter controversies of 1839-43, and the difficulties constantly encountered by the Committee of Council thereafter, made governments generally unwilling to risk arousing the passions which would accompany any parliamentary conflict, and although individuals and associations made repeated attempts up till 1868 to induce parliament to sanction fundamental changes, all were defeated. This was principally because of the two great obstacles presented by (a) the religious problem, and (b) the difficulty of arriving at agreement about local control should financial support for some new system of educational provision be drawn from local rates. In relation to the former, a particular hindrance arose from the fact that those who opposed the status quo and wished to alter or to supplement it could not agree among themselves as to what part (if any) existing schools should play in a different, more comprehensive scheme. Even more important, they were divided about whether any proposed new schools, being quite unconnected with the churches, should provide only secular teaching or permit some form of religious instruction.

Only a few examples of these parliamentary initiatives need be referred to here—chosen to throw light on the difficulties faced by those who framed the Act of 1870. Thus in 1850 the National Public School Association was established to promote through legislation the education policy of the Radicals—that elementary education should be provided wherever required, and be free, compulsory, supported from local rates and subject to local government control; after a significant dispute as to whether schools thus assisted should give only secular instruction, Richard Cobden, with the support of W. E. Forster, won the day for the proposal that unsectarian religious instruction might be permitted. Later the Association expressed willingness to allow rate aid for denominational schools if these became subject to local control; but this condition proved unacceptable. On the other hand, the rare government initiative represented by Lord John Russell's Bill of 1853, proposing that towns might spend rates on existing schools, was defeated, largely because no arrangements were envisaged for local representation.

Sir John Pakington, in 1855, introduced a Bill proposing the establishment, where desired, of local school boards, able to assist those existing schools willing to adopt a conscience clause, and to establish and support new schools in which the form of religious instruction (though subject to a conscience clause) would be in accordance with the creed most prevalent in the area. The Bill failed to win adequate support.

The Manchester Education Aid Society was established in 1864 to investigate and improve the educational provision in the city; it developed into the Manchester Education Bill Committee, which in 1867 and 1868 put forward Bills that were introduced in parliament by H. A. Bruce (a former vice-president of the Committee of Council), supported by W. E. Forster. These Bills proposed the provision everywhere of free and compulsory elementary education, supported from local rates, subject to local control and including unsectarian religious instruction; existing schools would receive financial aid if they adopted a conscience clause, but would not be subject to local control. This last provision aroused the particular hostility of many Radicals and Nonconformists, and helped to ensure the failure of the Bills. The failure was the more disappointing since in 1866 parliament had passed the Industrial Schools Act, which empowered local authorities to give assistance from the rates in respect of children attending the relatively small number of denominational industrial schools.

9 The Need for Action

With every year that passed during the 1860's it became more obvious that, however the obstacles were to be overcome, Britain could not long remain without a truly national system of elementary education. Competition from abroad in commerce and industry was becoming ever more keen, yet there did not exist in England and Wales a basis for producing a generally literate labour force, or a foundation on which to erect a comprehensive system of secondary, technical and commercial education. More parents were becoming anxious to send their children to school, especially as the usefulness of child labour, and therefore the demand for it, were diminishing. The rising influence of the socialist, secularist and trade union movements[17] aroused impatience over the angry disputes among clergymen which stood in the way of educational progress. With the considerable extension of the franchise in 1867, the need for more widespread provision for elementary education became still more evident to many; even Robert Lowe, the architect of the system of 'payment by results', became convinced that it was now necessary 'to compel our future masters to learn their letters'.[18]

Moreover it could no longer be denied that adequate development must involve greatly increased expenditure from public funds. The Voluntaryist movement, as we have noted, had set out more than twenty years earlier to prove the extreme Nonconformist case: that government aid for elementary education was wrong, unjust, pernicious and quite unnecessary; but in 1867 the movement collapsed and its leaders admitted total defeat in the face of hard economic facts.[19]

Even the principle that, except in most exceptional circumstances, parents must be expected to contribute towards the cost of their children's education was becoming untenable: bodies such as the Manchester Education Aid Society (founded in 1864) and the Birmingham Education Aid Society (founded in 1867) were finding that vast numbers of children would never attend school if their parents were obliged to pay any fee, however small. And since even those church schools which received government grants relied on fees for an average of about one-third of their annual expenditure (in some cases much more),[20] the limitations of existing methods of support were obvious.

The Newcastle Commission had complained that 'one of the chief failures' of the existing grant system was that it 'did not touch the districts which require most assistance'.[21] The state, acting upon the prevailing economic principles we have noted, favoured those most willing to help themselves; but willingness could be of little avail where resources were meagre. The amount of government grant (if any) depended upon the available voluntary contributions towards building and running costs, upon income from school fees, upon regular attendance, and upon adequate staffing and reasonable efficiency; therefore the districts least likely to have state-aided schools were precisely those where assistance was most required, because voluntary contributions were hard to obtain, qualified teachers could not be afforded, and parents were too poor or too feckless to pay for their children's schooling, to forgo income from children's labour, or to insist upon regular attendance at school. The system of 'payment by results' merely accentuated this position. The least efficient schools 'earned' the smallest grants, or none at all; but even if any impecunious school 'earned' a satisfactory state grant, only so much of this was actually paid as could be matched from the school's other resources, so that money which might have paid for an additional teacher or extra accommodation was simply withheld.

The voluntary organisations, in short, had not the resources to deal with the situation, especially as there were constant movements of population into the towns or from the centres of towns to the outskirts. In some parishes several competing schools might be set up by rival denominations whilst other comparable parishes had none. A further difficulty was that there was little provision for the children of the most destitute and brutalised inhabitants of the slums, since more 'respectable' working-class parents would often refuse to send their children to schools which admitted these. In the face of all this, the great weakness of the existing system was that, however much the state might augment expenditure on education and demand increased control, it had no power to *initiate* educational provision, to set up schools where they were seen to be required. The resulting situation in such places as Manchester and Liverpool in 1869 was clearly described by one experienced inspector:

> This class, or section of the population of these two large towns
> . . . which lies between the paupers and criminals on the one
> hand, and the independent and skilled working men on the
> other hand, is the one in which the greatest amount of educa-
> tional destitution exists, which has hitherto received the least
> amount of educational recognition and help from the nation,
> and for whose educational improvement the existing means are
> the most inadequate and defective. If a labourer of this class by
> sobriety, industry, and good fortune, rises into the ranks of
> foremen, or obtains steady employment and good wages, he will
> find excellent schools, maintained by voluntary effort and
> aided by public grants, in which his children will be taught by
> some of the most competent teachers in the country, and where
> he will only have to pay about one-third of the cost of their
> education. If, on the other hand, he gives up, or is beaten in the
> struggle for independence or honesty, and falls into the pauper
> or criminal class, here again the State will come to the assistance
> of his children, will rescue them, and contribute largely both
> to their maintenance and their education. But so long as he
> remains in the section which is neither wholly independent, nor
> yet quite pauper, he finds the provision made, whether by
> voluntary effort or by the State, for assisting him to educate his
> children, is wholly insufficient.[22]

10 Preparing for Battle

As it became clear that vital decisions must soon be taken, the opposing groups organised for combat. The controversy over the conscience clause had particularly embittered the Nonconformists, even the moderate Wesleyans. At this time, and for generations afterwards, conduct which the more inflexible Anglicans thought of as upholding the supremacy of spiritual over temporal affairs, as preserving the inseparable connection between secular and religious instruction, or more simply, as defending truth against error, was regarded by many Nonconformists merely as proof that the Church of England was much less concerned about education than about recruiting to its own ranks, with the aid of public funds[23] contributed by members of all sects, the children of poor Nonconformist or indifferent parents. And as those Anglicans most active in supporting their church and its schools were often also those known to be most given to 'Popish' doctrines, their attitude inspired determined resistance and uncompromising, angry repugnance. The Nonconformists and the Radicals were heartened when the Liberals, led by Gladstone, were returned to power in 1868 with an impressive majority. One Radical, W. E. Forster, who, as has been shown, had supported earlier attempts to extend educational provision, became vice-president of the Committee of Council on Education, in effect the minister responsible for the supervision of the existing system. In its first year the new government abolished the much-detested obligation to pay church-rates, and this made opponents of the Established Church the more determined that it should not now receive new financial support by way of rate aid for Anglican schools.

The organisation most active in its opposition to the expenditure of public money on denominational schools was the National Education League, founded in 1869 as a development of the Birmingham Education Aid Society. It advocated the establishment of a national system of elementary education, to be provided in non-denominational schools supported from local rates and subject to local control. Many of its members supported the Radical demand that such education should be free, compulsory and secular, but the majority advocated unsectarian religious instruction, either from personal conviction or from fear of alienating those who would be shocked at the omission of all religious instruction from the curricula of schools.

The chairman of the National Education League was George Dixon, an Anglican, and prominent members were Joseph Chamberlain, a Unitarian and a Radical, Dr R. W. Dale, a Congregationalist minister, and Dr H. W. Crosskey, a Unitarian minister. The two last were honorary secretaries of the Central Nonconformist Committee (established in 1870), which had close connections with the League and helped to co-ordinate support for its policies. The League campaigned very vigorously and made its influence felt throughout England; a comparable society, the Welsh Educational Alliance, was equally active in Wales. The general aims of the League found favour among people holding very different religious views and even with many indifferent or hostile to religion, so that the detailed definition of its policies gave rise to considerable divergences of opinion, as we shall see.

Naturally a rival body, the National Education Union, was founded to demand the continuance and extension of public financial support for denominational schools (now mainly Anglican and Roman Catholic, with some Wesleyan). Because such schools were so greatly dependent on parental fees, the Union opposed the abolition of these, except in the case of paupers and vagrants; and since the schools were in no position to cater for a sudden great increase in numbers, the Union was against the proposal to make school attendance compulsory, unless indirectly as a result of the extension of the Factory Acts, making employment conditional upon some evidence of attendance at school. On the other hand the Union was willing to accept a 'conscience clause' for state-aided schools, since the National Society had at last come to agree to this, in spite of the diehard opposition of some Anglicans.[24]

The Union had two great sources of strength. In the first place, its beliefs and purposes were very strongly supported in parliament, and particularly in the House of Lords. But much more important was the very existence of such great numbers of denominational schools: it would manifestly be difficult for any government, however doctrinaire, to frame policies which ignored the vast capital resources and moral determination represented by such schools, or the bargaining power held by those who owned them. However, those who supported denominational schools, like their opponents in the League, had their divisive differences of opinion. Protestants, and particularly Wesleyans, were often uncomfortably aware that the extension of denominational education would favour the spread of Roman Catholicism; even within the Protestant fold there were sharp sectarian disputes; whilst many Anglicans and Roman Catholics opposed the acceptance of rate aid because of the consequences that this would probably entail—some degree of local control and the imposition of a conscience clause.

11 The Parents[25]

The 'pressure groups' which strove to influence government policy in 1870 were many and strong, but little attention was paid to the views of the parents who sent their children to elementary schools. Their claims to be consulted might have been based not merely on parental rights but also on their contributions towards the cost of running the schools, since, according to Gladstone (as we shall see), the proportion of the annual income derived from school fees was roughly equal to that supplied by the state, and also to that provided by voluntary subscriptions, including those from religious communions. It would seem that most of the Roman Catholic parents wished their children to attend Roman Catholic schools, and that most other parents did not. It was generally agreed that, in spite of the efforts of secularists and some socialists among working men, there was a very widespread feeling in favour of Bible teaching in schools and against the prohibition of all religious instruction. But industrialisation and the movement of great populations to the towns had done much to break older ties where these had existed; the parish organisation of the Established Church had become largely ineffective; the church's close association with the ruling class had created much hostility and distrust; Nonconformity had tended to become 'respectable' and to make little appeal to the 'labouring classes', except in parts of Wales and in a few remote areas in England; there was widespread apathy and ignorance, in spite of sporadic efforts to conduct 'missions' in the slums.

C

Where the parents cared about education at all—and the contributions from fees showed that there were many such—they were mostly willing to ignore doctrinal differences and to seek the best schooling available for their children; though some quietly resented requirements such as compulsory attendance at a particular church, since these seemed to imply formal adherence to a given denomination. This 'comparatively passive attitude of the body of the people' (as the Newcastle Commission described it)[26] was of little importance whilst decisions did not lie in their hands: indeed it was a powerful challenge to the various religious groups, either because it inspired further missionary endeavour or, according to the point of view, gave those who controlled the religious instruction in the schools the opportunity to proselytise on a vast scale. But it was an attitude which was to have considerable importance later.

(Notes to this section are on pages 80-1)

SECTION TWO

PROBLEMS, DEBATES AND DECISIONS

1 Introduction

When the new Liberal government began to frame the Elementary Education Bill to be submitted to parliament in February 1870, some of the obstacles in the way of providing a national system of elementary education had been removed. It was now very widely agreed that the Church of England could no longer expect to receive more favourable treatment within such a system than was accorded to other churches; it was almost universally accepted that considerable expenditure of public funds would be required; and, however reluctantly, nearly all of those who favoured denominational religious instruction gave assent to the principle that, since rates and taxes were paid by those of all creeds and of none, withdrawal from such instruction on conscientious grounds must be permitted in schools aided from these sources. Above all, the conviction that a national system was needed was now more widespread than ever.

Nevertheless many of the problems which had daunted governments for decades seemed no nearer to solution than before. As in the case of the Reform Bill of 1832, and of the struggle leading to the repeal of the Corn Laws in 1846, the agitation outside parliament now had very great influence on what went on within it. Deep emotions were stirred both by the prospect of triumph and by the desperation born of approaching defeat. Moreover in 1870 the conflicting parties were divided among themselves, so that there was not only hostility towards opponents but resentment of what was taken to be treachery on the part of supposed friends.

Gladstone's cabinet seems to have approached its task in a most remarkable state of indecision, and this is not altogether surprising. The party derived much of its support from the Nonconformists and Radicals, yet the prime minister was a devout Anglican, whilst the only Radical in the cabinet, John Bright, was incapacitated by illness. The Vice-President of the Committee of Council on Education (and as such the de facto minister for educational affairs) was the Radical W. E. Forster; his nominal superior, the Earl de Grey and Ripon, Lord President of the Council (and spokesman for the government on the Bill in the House of Lords), was before long to become a Roman Catholic.

It may be convenient to consider the government's attempts to deal with its chief problems not in accordance with an estimated scale of difficulty or importance but, with some necessary variations, in the order in which they occur in the Act as passed.

2 Definitions

How was the field of elementary education, for the purposes of the Act, to be defined and limited? For whom would state-aided elementary schools be intended?

No attempt was made to specify what elementary education should consist of: probably this was considered unnecessary since, as in the past, regulations issued by the Committee of Council would from time to time indicate what subjects would 'earn' government grant in accordance with the system of 'payment by results'. It was not even required that an aided elementary school should provide only elementary education, since such a school was defined in the Act merely as one in which elementary education formed 'the principal part of the education there given'. (s 3). The intention was clearly to allow for more extension of the curriculum beyond the three R's; already, since 1867, the Revised Code had been modified to allow grants for one or two 'specific subjects' such as history and geography. As for the social status of the children to be catered for, the only stipulation was that the parental contribution must not exceed ninepence (4p) per week (ibid). The implications of this requirement will be considered later, but here it may be noted that the upper limit thus prescribed was, for the period, a remarkably high one.

3 The Supply of Schools

The debates in the Commons revealed a wide measure of agreement that many more schools must be provided. Forster claimed that 'only two-fifths of the children of the working classes between the ages of six and ten years . . . and only one-third of those between the ages of ten and twelve' were on the registers of the Government-aided schools, i e in schools inspected for grant

purposes. As for the schools not so inspected, these were 'generally speaking, the worst schools, and those least fitted to give a
good education to the children of the working classes.' A recent
survey,[1] he maintained, had indicated that 'in Liverpool the
number of children who ought to receive an elementary education is 80,000, but, as far as we can ascertain, 20,000 of them
attend no school whatever, while at least another 20,000 attend
schools where they get an education not worth having'; and comparable situations, he declared, existed in Birmingham, Leeds
and Manchester. (H., CXCIX, 441-2)

There was some disposition to challenge such figures, on the
grounds that the contribution of the uninspected schools had
been underestimated; that school populations were constantly
changing, so that many more children were being educated than
were in attendance at any one time; and that the Newcastle Commission had considered not eight but 'six years of schooling' adequate for children of the working classes. (H., CXCIX, 469)
Nevertheless it could hardly be denied that many thousands of
children who ought to have been in schools were roaming the
streets; and it was a Conservative member for Liverpool, Vis-
count Sandon, who urged the government to take powers to
acquire school sites by compulsory purchase where necessary.
(H., CXCIX, 481)

Given that the existing provision for elementary education was
manifestly inadequate, two sets of problems arose:

(i) What was to happen to the existing schools? Were they
to be (1) taken over by public bodies and assimilated into a
new system, or (2) allowed to remain in existence without
aid from public funds, or (3) given only such assistance as
they now received, or (4) provided with increased financial
support so that the voluntary organisations might be enabled to establish some or all of the additional schools required?
(ii) If the voluntary bodies were not to supply all of the new
schools, who should do so (1) under existing circumstances,
(2) when deficiencies occurred in the future? If public
authorities were to set up schools, should they do so in
all parts of the kingdom so that competition and choice became possible, or only in those localities where additional

schools were considered to be needed? Who should decide when and where new schools were required, and on what grounds?

Attempts to choose among these lines of policy gave rise to vehement controversy. Those who favoured denominational instruction sought the greatest possible extension of the existing system; most of their opponents, whether they hoped to abolish that system at once or merely wished to see it eventually fade away, were determined that no additional encouragement should be given to it, and that publicly owned and controlled schools should be made available in all parts of the country—especially in what had been, or might become, single-school areas.

But here the government was firm. The voluntary system must remain in being. Forster explained the principles on which future policy would be based:

> First of all, we must not forget the duty of the parents. Then we must not forget our duty to our constituencies, our duty to the taxpayers . . . And thirdly, we must take care not to destroy in building up—not to destroy the existing system in introducing a new one . . . Our object is to complete the present voluntary system, to fill up gaps, sparing the public money where it can be done without, procuring as much as we can the assistance of parents, and welcoming as much as we rightly can the co-operation and aid of those benevolent men who desire to assist their neighbours. (H., CXCIX, 443-4)

It was decided that the whole of Britain would be divided into 'school districts': generally speaking these would correspond with boroughs in urban areas and with civil parishes in rural places (but see the First Schedule to the Act for the detailed arrangements). In every school district there must be provided 'a sufficient amount of accommodation in public elementary schools . . . available for all the children resident in such district for whose elementary education efficient and suitable provision is not otherwise made.' (s 5) Forster defined his terms with remarkable vagueness: 'by efficient I mean schools which give a reasonable amount of secular instruction; and by suitable I mean schools to which, from the absence of religious or other restriction, parents cannot reasonably object'. (H., CXCIX, 445)

This explanation of the word 'suitable', indicating one of the factors to be taken into account when it was decided (then or in future) whether or not deficiency existed, was not written into the Act. (It was remarkably more evasive than the positive declaration in the current version of the Revised Code, which made it one condition for payment of grant 'that the religious denomination of the new school is suitable to the families relied upon for supplying scholars').[2] Forster offered to include in the Act the words

> And in considering whether a school is suitable or not, the Education Department shall have regard (among other matters) to the religious opinions of the inhabitants of such district. (H., CCII, 1113)

But he was obliged to withdraw his amendment in the face of objections to government enquiries into religious beliefs.

Where 'efficient and suitable' provision was not considered by the Education Department to be 'sufficient' it would be necessary, in Forster's words, to 'fill up gaps'. How was this to be done? After due enquiry and consideration of local objections the Department would issue a 'final notice' indicating what additional accommodation, if any, it considered to be needed in each district. If, within a period 'not exceeding six months' thereafter, the necessary accommodation had not been supplied, 'nor is in course of being supplied with due despatch', the Education Department would cause a school board to be set up, charged with making good the deficiency. (s 10) (The government had originally proposed that the 'period of grace' allowed should be one of twelve months, but opponents of the voluntary system had protested against the delay this would entail) .

The initiative to establish a school board might come from those entitled to elect such a board or, in a borough, from the council. (s 11) Boards could be set up, as they were considered to be needed, at any future time (s 13); and if a board did not provide schools as required, or otherwise contravened the regulations governing the supply and conduct of schools, the Education Department could declare the board in default and proceed to nominate persons to form a new board, the members of the defaulting board being 'deemed to have vacated their offices as if they were dead'. (s 63)

The powers of the boards were extensive. They were enabled to acquire sites for schools by compulsory purchase (s 20); to build and improve schools; to borrow money in order to do this (s 57); and to 'supply school apparatus and everything necessary

for the efficiency of the school'. (s 19) They could establish or
assist Industrial Schools. (ss 27, 28) They were permitted, under
certain conditions, to accept the transfer of existing voluntary
schools, and to re-transfer these later should the board so agree.
(ss 23, 24) Their powers respecting fees, rates and school attendance will be considered below. An important clause prescribed
that

> The school board . . . shall from time to time provide such
> additional school accommodation as is, in their opinion, neces-
> sary in order to supply a sufficient amount of public school
> accommodation for their district. (s 18)

This seemed clearly to imply, inter alia, that the decision
whether a new voluntary school was required (and therefore
would be eligible for grants if established) would be left to the
local school board in a district where one existed (but, manifestly, not elsewhere). Curiously enough, this crucial section was
barely discussed in parliament. One member moved in the Commons that the sanction of the Education Department should be
required before additional school accommodation was provided
by a board, since a board 'elected by a political or sectarian
party . . . might unnecessarily erect a school for their own purposes'; but the amendment was at once withdrawn when Forster
observed that 'he did not think a school board should always be
asking the sanction of the department'. (H., CCII, 1317)

A later section of the Act, however, stated that, where the
managers of any school within a school board district (whether
managers of a voluntary or of a board school) applied for parliamentary grant for the first time, the Education Department
might refuse such application 'if they think that such school is
unnecessary'. (s 98) Thus both sections left open the question of
applications in respect of new schools *not* in school board districts; whilst decisions as to necessity (and therefore as to eligibil-
ity for government grant) within school board districts were left
by one section to the school boards and by the other to the
Education Department. This confusion led to considerable controversy and legal argument later on.

School boards were authorised by the Act to delegate any of
their powers 'except the power of raising money'; in particular,
they might delegate the control and management of any school
provided by them to a body of managers appointed by them,

consisting of not less than three persons. It may be of interest to note that quite a heated debate took place before the following amendment was decisively rejected:

> In every such board school provision shall be made for giving to the parents of the children educated therein, and contributing thereto, a representation on the management of such schools . . .

4 The Constitution of School Boards

As we have seen, governments and many individuals anxious to extend educational provision had earlier wished to ensure that at least part of the expenditure on grants in aid of education should be provided from local rates; but parliamentary bills designed to ensure this had foundered, partly because of disputes over the degree and form of local control which might be demanded in return for local contributions. There was apprehension lest local control of any kind might lead to harsh treatment of voluntary bodies in some areas; in particular, many Roman Catholic and Nonconformist leaders were apprehensive, though some, including Cardinal Manning, had been re-assured by the working of the Industrial Schools Act of 1866, which appeared to have demonstrated that local authorities could be found who would fulfil their legal obligations to voluntary bodies without prejudice or bigotry.[3]

We have noted that a further difficulty was the absence of a national framework of efficient local government outside the larger towns and cities: Forster himself remarked, 'We are behind almost every other civilised country, whether in America or on the Continent of Europe, in respect to rural municipal organisation; and this drawback meets us not only in connection with education, but when many other social questions affecting the people come before us'. (H., CXCIX, 452)

The government had to choose between two policies. It could make use of the existing ramshackle system of vestries and select vestries (along with the more representative councils where these were to be found); or it could follow the precedents already set in relation to legislation concerning paupers, public health etc, and establish ad hoc boards for the purpose of carrying out the functions prescribed in the Act.

Forster first announced that the former policy would be adopted; but so intense was the opposition of the Nonconformists and Radicals (who, as has been shown, regarded the vestries as the local Conservative and Anglican bastions), that the proposal was quickly dropped in favour of the setting up of school boards where required. Special arrangements would be made for London, which would have one school board made up of representatives elected from ten 'divisions' of the metropolis. (s 37; Fifth Schedule) It was evident that problems would arise as to the relationship which should exist between a school board and the local government authority for the district, especially where the authority was a powerful borough council; in particular, the arrangements laid down concerning the levying and expenditure of rates caused considerable difficulty, as we shall see.

School boards, except in London, were to consist of five to fifteen members, elected in the boroughs by the burgesses and in parishes by the ratepayers. (s 29) An interesting and important provision was that at the elections (held triennially) each voter would be allowed to cast as many votes as there were members to be elected, and might 'give all such votes to one candidate, or . . . distribute them among the candidates, as he thinks fit'. (ibid) This meant that minorities could improve their chances of representation by agreeing to throw their combined voting strength in support of not more than a few chosen candidates. After a great deal of heated discussion it was agreed in the Commons that voting should be by ballot, in spite of the protest of one member that secret voting was 'contrary to the system which had been the honour and glory of England'. (H., CCIII, 303); however, this decision was reversed in the Lords, and voting by ballot was retained only for those districts of the metropolis which lay outside the City of London (secret voting for vestrymen having been inaugurated in those districts by the Metropolis Management Act of 1855).

5 Finance

Henceforth board schools and voluntary schools, if recognised as 'efficient', would have three broad sources of income: local rates or voluntary contributions, school fees, and government grants.

A   Local Rates or Voluntary Contributions

It is surprising to a modern student of history that these two very dissimilar sources of income should ever be equated or even bracketed together: yet to a great extent the rationale and the eventual practical operation of the 1870 Act depended upon their being so. Both were spoken of as resulting from 'local agency' (as during the parliamentary debates) or as the fruits of 'voluntary local exertion' (as in the formal *Minutes of the Committee of Council*, in which, before and after the passage of the Act, detailed regulations concerning grants were laid down).

As we have seen, proposals to finance elementary education from local rates had in the past given rise to great controversy. Apart from the common aversion to paying increased rates, there were conscientious objections to doing so in order to promote religious instruction (especially where this was considered erroneous); whether such instruction was unrestricted, limited, or prohibited, many ratepayers would feel aggrieved—and the use made of their payments would be more clearly seen than in the case of their contributions to general national taxation. Moreover there was the problem of the degree of control which ratepayers might require over the schools they supported.

Some of the solutions now proposed to meet these difficulties were discussed above when the constitution of the new school boards was described. The boards would not need to ask for voluntary contributions since, although they could not themselves levy a rate, they could require the local rating authority to do so: this division of power between those who were to spend the money and those who had the responsibility (and often the odium) involved in collecting it was to give rise to much difficulty and criticism later. The rating authorities were many and diverse: in almost all boroughs these were the local councils; in almost all parishes, the overseers of the poor; within the metropolis the authorities differed, that for the City of London being the Commissioners of Sewers. (First Schedule)

The chief difficulty arose from the fact that rates would be payable by members of all denominations (as of none), so that justice seemed to demand that voluntary as well as board schools should share the benefit. Forster reminded the House that he and H. A. Bruce (now Home Secretary) had, only a few years earlier, introduced Bills (on behalf of the Manchester Education Bill Committee) which included proposals that local school boards be compelled to assist voluntary schools from the rates. The government, however, did not now insist on compulsion. Instead, the school boards, it was suggested, would merely be *enabled* to aid voluntary schools if they so desired—with one important stipulation:

> They may either provide schools themselves, or assist the present schools, or they may do both. But there is this condition, that if they do go on the principle of assisting, they must assist all schools on equal terms. They may not pick out one particular denomination and say—"We shall assist you, but not the others". If they go on the principle of assistance, they must assist every public elementary school. (H., CXCIX, 456)

We have seen that the opposition to rate support for voluntary schools had caused numbers of parliamentary Bills to founder in the past, and on this occasion the great outcry from its own Nonconformist and Radical supporters quickly caused the government to change course. It decided that rate aid should *not* be given to voluntary schools. Apparently by oversight, a small loophole was left in the Act, as we shall see, but the general principle was accepted by the government—and this all the more readily because of the apprehension among some of those associated with voluntary schools lest rate support might lead to secular control.

Naturally, however, those who favoured voluntary schools were quick to point out that supporters of such schools would have to pay rates to maintain schools which they abhorred, in addition to making contributions to the schools they preferred to assist. One member of parliament proposed that rates otherwise payable might be reduced by the amount contributed to a voluntary school, but this suggestion received no support. (H., CCII, 1668) Indeed voluntary schools themselves were rated, and thus their managers would be obliged to contribute towards the support of rival institutions. And it may be convenient to note here two further departures from the declared principle that school boards and the managers of voluntary schools should receive equal treatment: the boards were empowered to acquire sites for schools by compulsory purchase (s 20), and to borrow money on the security of the rates (s 58), but no such powers were given to those who proposed to provide voluntary schools.

B School Fees

In his speech introducing the Bill, W. E. Forster declared that, when setting out 'to cover the country with good schools', the government would abide by certain conditions which it trusted would meet with the approval of members on both sides of the House. The first of these was that 'we must not forget the duty of the parents'; there must be 'the most careful absence of all encouragement to parents to neglect their children'. (H., CXCIX, 443) In fact it had become part of the programme of the National Education League to campaign for free elementary education as a corollary to making such education compulsory: the experience of Education Aid Societies in Birmingham, Manchester, Liverpool and elsewhere had shown clearly enough that very many parents were unwilling or unable to pay school fees. An Act of 1855 (18 and 19 Vict. c. 34) permitted boards of guardians to pay for the schooling of children of paupers receiving outdoor relief, but the results had proved unsatisfactory, because the powers were restricted, guardians were often unwilling to incur what they considered unreasonable expense,[4] and many parents were unwilling to be branded as paupers.

In 1870 the government was probably rather less concerned about parental duties than about the cost of dispensing with school fees. Forster observed:

> . . . shall we give up the school fees? I know that some earnest friends of education would do that. I at once say that the Government are not prepared to do it. If we did so the sacrifice would be enormous. The parents paid in school fees last year about £420,000. If this scheme works, as I have said we hope it will work, it will very soon cover the country, and that £420,000 would have to be doubled or even trebled. Nor would it stop there . . . The middle classes would step in—the best portion of the working classes would step in—and say "There must be free education also for us, and that free education must not be confined to elementary schools" . . . The cost would be such as really might well alarm my right hon. friend the Chancellor of the Exchequer. (H., CXCIX, 454)

But though he maintained that it would be 'not only unnecessary but mischievous' to 'relieve the parent from all payments for the education of his child', it was impossible to ignore the 'fearful educational destitution' that existed in 'large places like Liverpool or Manchester'. Therefore the government would give the school board power to establish special free schools under special circumstances, which chiefly apply to large towns, where, from the exceeding poverty of the district, or for other very special reasons, they prove to the satisfaction of the government that such a school is needed . . . We require the approval of the Government . . . upon the ground that it would not be fair to the existing schools to allow a free school to be set up unless on very special grounds. (H., CXCIX, 455)

As a further concession, the Act empowered the school board, 'if they think fit', to 'pay the whole or any part of the school fees payable at any public elementary school by any child resident in their district whose parent is in their opinion unable from poverty to pay the same'. It was expressly stated in the Act that 'such payment shall not be deemed to be parochial relief given to such parent'. No payment of school fees was to be made or refused by a school board 'on condition of the child attending any public elementary school other than such as may be selected by the parent.' (s 25) Clearly one result of this section was that there would be no such provision for assistance in paying school fees in districts where no school board existed; another that (in spite of earlier decisions) money provided from rates could become part of the income of voluntary schools; yet a school board could refuse to make use of its powers so long as no conditions were overtly expressed. These implications went almost unnoticed for a time, but later they aroused extraordinarily bitter controversy.

Several other aspects of the government's policy regarding parental contributions deserve attention. In the first place, as noted earlier, the maximum fee chargeable in a grant-aided school of ninepence per week (4p) was to be set very high in relation to fees normally paid in such schools hitherto. In grant-aided schools in 1869 about ninety per cent of children paid less than fourpence (2p) per week and less than three per cent more than fourpence. A quarter (almost half in Roman Catholic schools) paid less than twopence (1p).[5] The version of the Revised Code in force when the Act was passed declared bluntly that 'the object of the grant is to promote the education of children belonging to the classes who support themselves by manual labour';[6] other children might attend state-aided schools but no grant would be payable in respect of them. Not surprisingly, therefore, one member of parliament now 'thought it would be desirable to limit to the working classes the power of sending children to the elementary schools to be established under the Bill'; he moved that no parent should be entitled to send a child to a rate-aided school 'whose net income shall amount to £150 per annum'. There was no discussion of this proposal after Forster observed that 'in many cases there might be considerable advantage in having children of all classes attending the same school.' (H., CCII, 1265)

The level of the school fee chargeable was important not only because it implied that grant-aided schools would be available for children whose parents' incomes differed very considerably, but also for another reason, which was thought to involve a significant principle. In the eyes of many the whole case for allowing some state-aided schools to remain, in effect, exclusively denominational and largely controlled by the churches, depended on the fact that an appreciable part of the expenditure was met from voluntary contributions made by supporters of particular denominations: this, so to speak, 'earned' the right to give denominational instruction. But if the fees paid by parents (who might be of any creed or of none) were high enough, these, when added to the grants from public sources, might defray the whole annual cost of running the school and weaken the justification for its promoting the beliefs of a particular denomination.

It is not easy to establish what was the true cost, on average, of educating a child in a voluntary state-aided elementary school at this time: there was a tendency not to take into account loss of interest on capital expended or the value of sites given free by landowners, and it is not always apparent whether averages quoted are based on the numbers of children on a school register or of those in actual attendance. But it seems clear that a fee of 9d per week, in practice about £1 13s 0d (£1.65) per annum, would have met the costs of the *average* voluntary school, probably even without support from public funds, and certainly, given this, without the need for voluntary contributions. In 1861 the Report of the Newcastle Commission had sternly declared:

As the whole [average] expense of the education of each child is about £1 10s 0d [£1.50] a year, including the share of grants for teachers and central [i e government] office expenses, and as the attendance of the children lasts at the utmost for only 44 weeks in the year, no parent can be said to pay fully for the education of his child unless he pays at least 8d per week. The difference between what he actually pays and 8d a week is in the nature of a charitable donation. (1, 73)

During the debates on the Act, Gladstone, as we shall see, accepted this annual average of £1 10s 0d, though Forster, in a manner which typified the frequent lack of co-ordination between the two government spokesmen, later described this estimate as 'exaggerated' and considered the 'real cost'[7] to be £1 5s 7d (£1.28). (H., CCII, 1635)

Gladstone acknowledged the force of the argument for requiring voluntary contributions for church schools, and he gave a definite undertaking:

> We shall . . . take care that, under no circumstances, shall the public grants be allowed so to operate as entirely to supply, together with school pence, the sum necessary to support those schools, and that there shall always remain a void which must be filled up by free private contributions, and without which, failing other sources of assistance, those schools would no longer deserve the character of voluntary. (H., CCII, 938)

Yet a few weeks later Forster was refusing to concede such a pledge, as if ignorant that one had already been given:

> . . . they found that some of the best schools got on without voluntary subscriptions, because the parents were willing to pay larger fees. There was a Wesleyan school at the south side of London to which there were no voluntary subscriptions, but while the grant to that school was £205, the school pence amounted to £372. He found that several of the British schools, some Roman Catholic schools, and some Church schools—but a larger number which were not either Church schools or Roman Catholic schools—were in that position. Were the Government to say that these schools were not to have any grant because the parents were prepared to pay more than parents usually did pay, and there were no voluntary subscriptions? (H., CCIII, 87-8)

Gladstone's assurance was apparently forgotten; the Act merely required that the parliamentary grant should not exceed the total income of the school 'from voluntary contributions, and from school fees, and from any sources other than the parliamentary grant.' (s 97)

C   Government Grants

(a) Building Grants

Since 1833, as we have noted, parliament had provided funds to pay part of the cost of building some elementary schools. It

D

was now decided that such grants must cease. This decision had originally formed no part of the government's policy as expounded in Forster's introductory speech, but seems to have resulted from representations made to Gladstone by a deputation from the Wesleyan Methodists three months after the Bill had been introduced. Since 1847 the Wesleyans had readily accepted government grants towards the cost of building schools: they had declined to adopt the views of the Voluntaryists. But now they felt drawn to ally themselves more closely with the policies of other Nonconformists because of the long-maintained refusal of the Church of England to sanction officially the conscience clause, and because of their own reluctance to encourage the spread of any 'Romanising' influence, whether in Roman Catholic or (as they feared) in some Anglican schools. According to one Wesleyan leader, when the Wesleyans therefore objected on conscientious grounds to the continuance of building grants for denominational schools, 'Mr Forster gave way on this point almost immediately'.[8] Gladstone announced this highly important change of policy somewhat cursorily and with an extremely dubious justification:

> The building of schools is the easiest of all the efforts made by the promoters. Their great difficulty is the maintenance of the schools; and when we give liberal assistance to the maintenance, I think we may fairly leave to the locality the cost of the building. (H., CCII, 281)

The blow would be softened in two ways. Firstly, building grants would continue to be paid in respect of new schools for which plans were submitted before the end of 1870, if the plans were approved by the Education Department (s 96); because of this provision the last government grant in aid of building was in fact not made until 1881.[9] The second concession, concerned with annual grants, was of doubtful value, as we shall see.

(b) Annual Grants

The detailed conditions governing entitlement to annual parliamentary grants, and the amounts payable, were not specified in the Act: they were to be 'contained in the minutes of the Education Department in force for the time being.' (s 97) (In practice this meant, inter alia, that the contributions from the government would depend upon 'payment by results', capitation grants, etc, as under the existing system). However, it was considered necessary to spell out in the Act some general principles; those relating to the 'religious difficulty' will be discussed later, but two others are relevant here:

(i) It was a long standing principle, duly enshrined in the current Revised Code, that, however much a school might 'earn' by results or become entitled to in other ways, the parliamentary grant must not exceed the sum raised from 'voluntary local exertion' (including school fees) and other sources. This provision continued to form part of the Code after the Act was passed, it being understood that 'voluntary local exertion' would now, in the case of board schools, include income derived from rates. The Act formally emphasised the principle that the parliamentary grant 'shall not for any year exceed the income . . . derived from voluntary contributions, and from school fees, and from sources other than the parliamentary grant'. (s 97) There was a proviso however. In districts where a threepenny (1p) rate would produce annually less than £20 or 7s 6d (37½p) per child, the government grant to a school board which had expended such a sum in respect of any of its schools would be increased by the amount required to make good the deficit (up to that sum). Gladstone was convinced that this saving clause would not come into operation, since, in point of fact, 'the rate would never come to 3d in the pound'; moreover, in view of a proposed increase in government aid (to be discussed below), 'they might altogether dispense with this contingent reserve of assistance from the Exchequer . . . which the Government consider to be quite unnecessary under the circumstances'. (H., CCII, 280-1) The clause, nevertheless, remained part of the Act. (s 97)

(ii) In spite of this 'saving clause' and—more important— the rather questionable procedure of equating voluntary contributions with support from the rates, the general principle was laid down that the regulations governing the award of state grants 'should not give any preference or advantage to any school on the ground that it is or is not provided by a school board'. (ibid)

It will be remembered that, in the face of strong opposition from within and outside parliament, the government had modified its original financial plans in two important ways: it had withdrawn the proposal that school boards might assist voluntary schools from the rates (apart from assisting necessitous parents to pay fees) and it had decided that grants in aid of school building should cease. There was therefore some obligation to increase the financial support made available by the Exchequer for voluntary schools. The new provision was not included in the Act, but the government undertook that it would form part of subsequent issues of the Revised Code. Gladstone's discussion of the arrangement was confused and confusing. He said:

> I do not know whether the House is aware of the computations generally current as to the expenses of schools and the contributions to them. I believe that none of these computations can be said to be exact; but, speaking roughly, it is said that the expense of educating a child in an efficient secular school is 30s. [£1.50], of which it may be said one-third is now provided by the Privy Council, one-third from voluntary sources, and one-third by payments from the children. We think that if to the third which is now dispensed [i e by the Privy Council] the half of the second third [i e hitherto supplied from voluntary sources] were added . . . the voluntary schools would have no reason to complain.

He thought that justice would be done if there were 'an addition to the present grant from the Privy Council to the voluntary schools, which may be taken at its maximum of 50 per cent.' (H., CCII, 280) Since voluntary and board schools must be treated alike, the increased grant would be made available also to the latter.

There were several extraordinary features about this 'concession', arising partly from the failure to distinguish between average and maximum payments. In the first place, raising the maximum amount *obtainable* would not have altered the situation for the vast majority of schools, since the amount *actually* paid would continue to depend upon income from other sources and on 'payment by results'; relatively few schools were currently eligible for the maximum grant. As a puzzled correspondent wrote to one member of parliament:

> We are at a loss to know what Mr Gladstone means by saying he will increase the Government grant 50 per cent. Do please ask if possible . . . He is not really increasing the terms . . . but leaving it stationary with most schools, and only making its maximum attainable in others. So that we have little to be thankful for. (H., CCII, 1100)

Secondly, the current average expenditure for each child in attendance was said to be £1 10s 0d (£1.50), towards which the *average* state contribution was 10s (50p); and Gladstone was indicating that the government would increase its total grant by 50 per cent in raising the *maximum* state contribution to 15s (75p). But in fact the maximum was *already* 15s, as it had been since 1862. Only if the *average* state payment had been raised to 15s would the 50 per cent increase have operated. One Wesleyan leader later complained that Gladstone's speech on this occasion showed him to be 'not at all clear in his own understanding of the case . . . he did not understand . . . that, in fact, his possible maximum was not raised by a penny . . . [his] misconception on this point was peculiarly unfortunate'.[10] Yet no correction was made.

6 School Attendance

The government had rejected the claim that elementary education should be provided free: would it now accept another demand of the Radicals and of the National Education League by making school attendance compulsory? There was considerable opposition to compulsion among the supporters of voluntary schools, which could not possibly cope with a vastly increased need for places; we have noted that the National Education Union had rather reluctantly agreed that *indirect* compulsion (requiring evidence of school attendance as a condition of acceptance for some kinds of employment) might be acceptable. Opponents of compulsion claimed, among other things, that it was morally wrong, savoured of Prussian autocracy, would diminish the freedom of parents (making them irresponsible), and would deprive poor parents of the financial support of their children. One member of parliament even quoted Matthew Arnold (somewhat out of context) to maintain that growing up in England was in itself an education without parallel. (H., CCII, 1723)

Forster described himself as newly converted to a belief in compulsion, rejected the notion that it was 'un-English', and 'agreed that before long the principle of compulsion would probably be acknowledged'. (H., CCII, 1734-5) But until the necessary schools were available, and public opinion had come to accept the policy, the government would leave the matter to the judgment of each individual school board wherever one was established. The Act therefore empowered, but did not compel, school boards to make byelaws 'requiring the parents of children of such age, not less than five years nor more than thirteen years, as may be fixed by the byelaws, to cause such children (unless there is some reasonable excuse) to attend school.' (s 74)

7 The Religious Problem

This, of course, was the greatest difficulty of all, the one which, for more than a generation, had done most to hinder progress towards a national system of elementary education. The various claims and counter-claims, arguments and counter-arguments, had been so frequently fought over, and were still so vehemently advanced, that the government certainly could not have come forward with a generally acceptable programme; but it was hardly likely to meet with unexpected demands or surprising opposition, and it might have been expected to decide on its line of policy and be prepared to pursue this with some resolution. This was far from being the case.

A The Voluntary Schools

The government's decision to keep the voluntary schools in being was, on political and economic grounds, probably unavoidable. But two additional steps were not so, and were of the greatest importance. Firstly, by positively encouraging the further development of the voluntary system and providing grants (even if over a limited period) towards the cost of building new schools, it induced the voluntary bodies to undertake fresh commitments, and therefore tacitly accepted a continuing moral obligation towards them. Secondly, by refusing to accede to demands that school boards should be set up in *all* districts, it obliged parents in many places to send their children to voluntary schools; and frequently a voluntary school attached to a particular denomination would be the only one available.

We have seen that the government had pledged itself to ensure that 'suitable' schools would be available for all children, and that Forster had defined this (not within the Act) as meaning 'schools to which, from the absence of religious or other restrictions, parents cannot reasonably object'. (H., CXCIX, 445) Clearly the minimum safeguard which could fulfil this undertaking was the formal acceptance by those voluntary bodies in receipt of public aid of the right of parents to withdraw their children from religious instruction and observances. Hitherto, as was pointed out above, the government had insisted upon the inclusion of a 'conscience clause' in the trust deeds of all new schools to be built with aid from government grants in what would become single-school areas; the present requirement was far more important, since it would apply to *all* schools receiving *annual* state grants (whether board or voluntary schools). At first the government created great difficulties for itself by proposing that the parent could ensure withdrawal 'by sending his objection in writing'—obviously an additional deterrent for illiterate or poorly educated parents already hardly likely to wish to incur criticism from influential school managers or neighbours. The government was obliged by the determined opposition of large numbers of its own supporters not only to withdraw this stipulation but to introduce a 'time-table clause', that is, one requiring that any religious observance or religious instruction must take place at the beginning and/or at the end of a school meeting (s 7), so that withdrawal could be facilitated without loss of secular instruction.

The government now wished to adopt a neutral role, occupying itself only with the provision of secular education and not concerning itself with differences of religious belief. This was to be demonstrated in several ways:

(i) As we have already seen, the Act prescribed that 'the conditions required to be fulfilled by an elementary school in order to obtain an annual parliamentary grant' must not 'give any preference or advantage to any school on the ground that it is or is not provided by a school board'. (s 97) True, there were in practice numerous departures from this theoretical standpoint: for example there was the contingency clause, discussed above, which ensured increased grant for board schools when rate-aid fell below a certain level, and the provision that school boards might acquire sites for schools by compulsory purchase (s 20), whilst voluntary bodies could not. Other examples will be noted later. Nevertheless the general principle was considered by the government to be both practicable and important.

(ii) It was laid down that no grant-aided school might require, as a condition of admission, that any child must 'attend, or abstain from attending, any Sunday School, or any place of religious worship, or that he shall attend any religious observance or any instruction in the school or elsewhere'. (s 7)

(iii) The state grant would not be paid 'in respect of any instruction in religious subjects'. (s 97)

(iv) The grant would no longer be confined to schools which provided religious instruction. This was an important departure from the policy followed ever since state grants were first made available in 1833. From time to time the precise requirements concerning religious instruction had been modified to meet the scruples of the various religious bodies whose schools became eligible for grants: thus the reading of the Authorised Version of the Bible ceased to be obligatory when grants were made in respect of Roman Catholic schools. But the principle was strictly maintained, and in 1853 state aid was refused to the Williams's Secular School, Edinburgh, on the ground that the principle was 'in accordance with the will of the country' (the decision was published in the official *Minutes of the Committee of Council*[11] with the obvious purpose of confirming the rule and discouraging other applicants). The version of the Revised Code current when the Act was passed laid it down that

Every school aided from the grant must be either
(a) A school in connexion with some religious denomination; or (b) A school in which, beside secular instruction, the Scriptures are read daily from the authorised version. [12]

Now these stipulations were swept away: the conditions for obtaining the state grant would not 'require that the school shall be in connexion with a religious denomination, or that religious instruction shall be given in the school'. (s 97)

(v) The parliamentary debates produced further evidence that the government was determined to dissociate itself from the policies of the different religious groups within the field of elementary education. It was announced that the agreements with the various religious authorities recognising their right to be consulted when Her Majesty's Inspectors of Schools were appointed would now come to an end. Hitherto this right had generally led to appointments being made partly on a denominational basis. Moreover, as was shown earlier, the 'Concordat' of 1840 with the Church of England had gone much further, since, among other concessions, it had authorised inspectors of Anglican schools alone to examine religious as well as secular instruction, one practical consequence being that inadequacy in the former might result in partial or total loss of grant for the latter. Forster justified the ending of all such agreements by claiming that the insistence on denominational qualifications for inspectors prevented the most economical arrangement of their activities: he further observed that to permit state inspection of religious teaching in Church of England schools was unfair to members of other denominations, and could be unjust even to Anglicans whose religious views differed from those of a particular inspector. There were heated protests from some members of the Established Church at this unilateral abrogation of the 'Concordat', but the government stood firm, and the Act plainly declared that henceforth it would be no part of the duties of an inspector 'to inquire into any instruction in religious subjects.' (s 7)

B The Board Schools

The most difficult and controversial of all the questions which the government was called upon to answer were, (a) whether religious education of any kind should be given in the board schools, and (b) if so, what form it should take. Around these two questions crystallised the doctrinal and professional antagonisms of church leaders: on the one side, all the passionate belief in the importance of religious teaching as an integral part of school instruction, and, on the other side, strong convictions about the impossibility of reaching agreement on its form, about the impropriety of secular authorities 'meddling' with religion, and about the injustice considered to be involved in using public funds to sustain the Church of England, or else (in the words commonly used later) to 'put Popery on the rates'.

The government's reply to both of the questions was simple, though, as soon appeared, hardly disarmingly so. We have noted that the decision whether or not to support voluntary schools from the rates had initially been left to the individual school boards. Similarly it was at first intended that the separate boards would be allowed to decide what religious instruction, if any, should be given in the schools they controlled. Forster asked the rhetorical question 'Ought we to restrict the school boards, in the matter of religion, more than we do the managers of voluntary schools?' and he replied, 'We have come to the conclusion that we ought not'. (H., CXCIX, 457) In other words, school boards could arrange to provide as much or as little religious instruction as they wished (or none at all) being bound only by the requirements of the 'time-table conscience clause'.

This was a proposal certain to arouse opposition on all sides, since it would alienate all those who favoured religious instruction (of whatever kind) by permitting the board schools to give purely secular instruction, and also all those who advocated purely secular instruction, since it permitted religious instruction of one sort or other. There would be the additional, not inconsiderable, difficulty of placating those who demanded the provision of religious instruction, should their preferred form of instruction not be adopted by their local boards. (The proposal to leave decisions about religious instruction to 'local option' was not new. In 1850 W. J. Fox had introduced a Bill which included provision for leaving questions concerning religious instruction to be decided by the ratepayers; Sir John Pakington's Bill in 1855 had proposed that religious teaching might be in accordance with the dominant creed of each locality).

The problem was a real one. Whatever regulations were made would have to be enforced, and Forster maintained that the task would be one of 'detailed supervision', which did not 'belong to the central government, and in which the great probability is the central government would fail.' On the other hand, he explained (making rather considerable assumptions in the process), members of the school board would be elected by the parents and therefore trusted by them: parents would be careful 'to elect men that will not raise difficulties in the way of religion'. (H.,

CXCIX, 458, 459) Others were less sanguine, foreseeing religious or irreligious intolerance given free play throughout the land, and rising to a peak when school board elections were fought. Eventually the proposal had to be withdrawn: Forster observed that deputations from metropolitan vestries and from the Manchester town council had asked that 'absolute discretion should not be left to them,' and it was evident 'that that was the feeling prevalent throughout the country'. (H., CCII, 1249) The ball was back in the government's court.

If the state were to insist upon some line of action, it could hardly, at this date, demand the provision of some one form of denominational instruction: the choice must therefore lie between permitting only secular instruction or prescribing some form of religious instruction which might be described as unsectarian.

The 'secular' solution had for decades attracted those Nonconformists who deplored state interference in religious affairs or financial support for rival denominations; it appealed to many who had no religious beliefs; and it was favoured by those impatient with the delays caused by disputes among the more committed members of the various religious communions. Yet there could be little real co-operation among those who supported the policy whilst themselves holding firm religious beliefs, and those who considered such beliefs to be foolish and harmful. Moreover, in spite of some growth in the influence of socialist and secularist movements among workmen, there was a widespread conviction that the parents of children attending elementary schools, whilst generally more interested in secular than in denominational education, were in favour of Bible-teaching in schools.

Because of his awareness that 'politics is the art of the possible', Cobden had in 1850 persuaded the newly formed National Public School Association to omit the word 'secular' from its title and, as we have seen, to propose that unsectarian religious instruction be permitted in the schools it was hoped to establish. Similarly the National Education League, though many of its members favoured purely secular education, now uneasily campaigned rather for unsectarian instruction so as not to alienate many potential supporters, particularly among Nonconformists. Forster himself pointed out that a deputation from Welsh Non-

conformist ministers had favoured 'secular, unsectarian' instruction, and a Welsh member of parliament had 'frankly confessed
that there was a difference of opinion . . . and it was thought
that by using the two words they might get over the difficulty'.
(H., CXCIX, 1936-7)

Forster summed up the position as follows:

> Why do we not prescribe that there shall be no religious teach-
> ing? Why, if we did so, out of the religious difficulty we should
> come to the irreligious difficulty. We want, while considering
> the rights and feelings of the minority, to do that which the
> majority of the parents in this country really wish; and we have
> no doubt whatever that an enormous majority of the parents of
> this country prefer that there should be a Christian training for
> their children—that they should be taught to read the Bible . . .
> Would it not be a monstrous thing that the Bible . . . should be
> the only book that was not allowed to be used in our schools?
> (H., CXCIX, 457-8)

Gladstone himself would have been prepared to accept the
'secular solution', leaving religious instruction to be given outside school hours by teachers, parents or ministers. He wrote, 'We
might have fallen back upon the plan of confining the rate to
secular subjects' (as indeed was to be the case with the government grant); 'but this was opposed by the church, the opposition,
most of the dissenters, and most of our own friends'.[13] The upshot
of all this was clear: there would be no compulsion to give religious instruction in board schools, but neither would religious
instruction be forbidden.

There remained the possibility of prescribing by law that if
religious instruction were to be given in board schools it must
be unsectarian. But in November 1869, when Gladstone had first
read Forster's memorandum outlining possible provisions for the
Bill, he had written to the Earl de Grey and Ripon (Forster's
superior as being President of the Council and therefore of the
Committee of Council on Education):

> I have read Forster's able paper, and I follow it very generally.
> On one point I cannot well follow it: the proposal to found
> the rate schools on the system of the British and Foreign Society
> would, I think, hardly do.[14]

On this point Gladstone had long held strong views, and he
maintained them into old age. His government would have
nothing to do with 'unsectarian' religious instruction. As voiced
by Forster in parliament, its opposition was based chiefly on three

arguments: (a) that there was no need to restrict the form of religious instruction, since the young children concerned would be incapable of being influenced by doctrinal differences, and in practice teachers would appreciate this; (b) that there could be no satisfactory agreement as to what would constitute unsectarian teaching—it would be impracticable to forbid, for example, explanation of biblical passages; and (c) that no definition could be found capable of being given legal force in an Act of Parliament. Gladstone stressed all of these, and in particular was scornful of the possibility of imposing unsectarian teaching 'to be limited and defined on appeal by a new sort of Pope in the Council Office'.[15]

Yet the policy laid down in the Act has been very widely misunderstood because of the government's agreement to embody in it the amendment relating to board schools proposed by W. F. Cowper-Temple: that 'No religious catechism or religious formulary which is distinctive of any particular denomination shall be taught in the school'. (s 14) Cowper-Temple, the chairman of the National Education Union and one of the chief spokesmen of those who favoured denominational instruction, was not the man to come forward as the champion of unsectarian instruction in board schools. His concern was to answer the complaint that certain books and prescribed forms of words were so closely associated with a particular religious communion that their use by children or teacher might in itself seem to imply acceptance of membership of that communion. As Forster said, there was 'an objection in the country to catechisms and special formularies . . . not so much on account of the actual words, but because the putting of them into the hands of children appeared to be like claiming those children as belonging to a particular Church'. He readily agreed that 'you may have sectarian teaching without sectarian formularies and catechisms'. (H., CCII, 1251, 590) Similarly Cowper-Temple himself explained that 'the exclusion of catechisms and formularies . . . dealt only with lesson books which bore upon their title-page plain indications of their origin'; he was decidedly opposed to any measures which would 'deprive the teachers in the schools created under the Bill, of the right, which everybody else in this country enjoyed, to explain the Bible according to his own views and opinions'. (H., CCII, 1276-7; CCIII, 739)

Gladstone made the attitude of the government quite plain:

> it is our wish that the exposition of the Bible in schools should take its natural course; that it should be confined to the simple and devout method of handling which is adapted to the understanding and characters of children; but we do not admit that the simple and devout character of teaching can be secured by an attempt to exclude all references to tenets and doctrines. That is an exclusion which cannot be effected, and, if it could, it ought not to be; it is an invasion of the freedom of religious teaching such as ought not to be tolerated in this country. (H., CCII, 1256)

The Prime Minister later assured a questioner that there must be 'free exposition of the Scriptures open to every schoolmaster who may be conscientiously attached to the Nonconformist community, subject, of course, as I hope he will be, to the restraints of commonsense, but to no other restraints of a legal kind'. (H., CCIII, 748) (It may be noted in passing that there was some inconsistency here, since the original plan of leaving decisions about religious instruction to school boards would certainly have limited the freedom of many teachers).

The rejection of a prescribed 'unsectarian solution' was made still more definite when Jacob Bright proposed an amendment designed to ensure that in a board school the religious instruction should not 'be used or directed in favour of or against the distinctive tenets of any religious denomination'. (H., CCII, 1271) Many of the government's own supporters argued and voted for the amendment, but the government successfully opposed it, with the support of large numbers of the opposition.

Yet the proposed solutions to the 'religious problem' embodied in the Act were not as clear-cut as they seemed. There was, of course, no doubt that voluntary schools might give denominational instruction, subject to permitting withdrawal at agreed times. In the board schools the decision had been taken out of the hands of the school boards: their sole responsibility in this matter would be to see that the prohibition of 'distinctive' catechisms and formularies was observed. It would be easy enough to recognise catechisms (which were used only in Church of England and Roman Catholic schools), but what would constitute a distinctive formulary? In spite of Gladstone's scorn for 'a new type of Pope in the Council office', decisions would clearly lie with the central Education Department. The government had rejected any other limitation of the freedom, in this sphere, of individual teachers, but had not in the Act defined their position. It had not even protected them from religious tests imposed by school boards anxious to recruit teachers of a given persuasion or of none; an amendment designed to give such protection was rejected by the government as 'unnecessary'. (H., CCII, 1046) Since most teachers had been trained in various denominational colleges (by far the greater proportion being Anglican) it appeared likely that the 'religious problem' would be transferred from parliament to the classroom. This was the real point of Disraeli's often quoted remark: 'You will not intrust the priest or the presbyter with the privilege of expounding the Holy Scriptures to the scholars; but for that purpose you are inventing and establishing a new sacerdotal class'. (H., CCII, 289)

The arguments based on principles and on the need for legal definitions were formidable: after all, even the 'unsectarian' teaching of the British and Foreign Society's schools was objected to by Roman Catholics, High Churchmen and Unitarians. But there was a strong body of opinion which believed that the vast majority of the parents most concerned had little interest in doctrinal differences, and that the 'religious problem' would, in practice, be no problem in the classroom. It was 'a very great political, parliamentary and polemical difficulty; but . . . not an educational difficulty' (Forster, H., CCII, 580); 'it was a difficulty which existed more in this House than out of it' (A. J. Mundella, H., CC, 243); when a group of practising teachers were consulted they agreed that the problem was 'only a platform difficulty'.[16] Gladstone, expressing a view which he had long held, was anxious to protect the freedom of conscience of the individual teacher, come what may, and even if his supporters were outraged. But Forster's outlook was less exalted, more practical:

My full belief is that, though it makes a good deal of difference in the passing of the Bill, yet, in working the Bill, it matters very little how we word this clause, provided we do not prescribe secular education; because, in the majority of cases, the local boards would establish schools very much upon the system of the British and Foreign School Society. It is upon this principle that schools are established by Englishmen, when they meet together as Englishmen, and not as members of a particular sect. (H., CCII, 589-90)

8 The Education Department

One result of the Act was to give to the Education Department very extensive powers. Henceforward its regulations, after lying for one month on the table of both Houses, would have the force of law. It would lay down conditions relating to government grants as in the past; but in addition it could now order enquiries as to school provision, decide whether or not school boards should be established (or discontinued), declare boards to be in default, and nominate new members to them. Its sanction was required concerning the level of school fees (including those in state-aided voluntary schools), the provision of free schools, borrowing for school building and extension, the transfer of schools to and from school boards, and the compulsory purchase of sites (though for this a special Act of Parliament was also required). (s 20) Its approval had to be sought respecting time-tables, and bye-laws concerning compulsory attendance; it could decide whether or not new schools were 'necessary' and therefore eligible for grant (though, as we have seen, there was some confusion here concerning the rights of school boards); and it had the task of ensuring that the 'conscience' and the 'Cowper-Temple' clauses were respected.

Yet, in spite of the representations of Earl Russell, A. J. Mundella and others, there was no provision to 'establish the office of a Minister of Education.' Gladstone was opposed to such a step, and years later Forster ruefully declared, 'The real objection probably is that it is undesirable to make too much of education. If we were to have a minister of education, he might be pushing things on too quickly'.[17]

(Notes to this section are on pages 81-2)

SECTION THREE

THE WORKING OF THE ACT

E

1 First Reactions

It is, of course, a feature of the political system in Britain that, not infrequently, a government will rely on the support of its parliamentary opposition in order to promote or resist a policy, despite criticism from many of its own supporters. The government assumes (sometimes mistakenly) that these critics will be politically impotent since, however frustrated they may feel, they will hardly themselves combine with the opposition; as the phrase is, 'they will have nowhere else to go.' This is an arrangement which permits a considerable amount of effective action to be taken in an atmosphere full of bitter denunciations and declarations of diehard resistance to 'betrayals' of the principles of the party concerned. Since we must here confine our attention to the practical working of the Act of 1870 we cannot study in any detail the reactions of the various political and religious groups except insofar as they influenced the operation of the Act.[1]

Most of those who favoured the voluntary system were relieved at the outcome of the parliamentary struggle. Though the Bishop of Lincoln feared that the time-table conscience clause would lead to the rise of a race of godless teachers and infidel scholars (H., CCIII, 1170), the widespread and well-organised agitation of the Education League had led such influential leaders as the Archbishop of York and the Earl of Shaftesbury to feel that a session's delay in passing the Bill would have had dire results for the Church of England. (H., CCII, 541 and CCIII, 1168) The Roman Catholics were guardedly ready to accept the Act, though apprehensive about many points, such as the likely absence of Roman Catholic teaching in board schools (to which many poor parents might be induced to send their children because of a remission of fees), the inability to acquire sites by compulsory purchase, and so on. (H., CCIII, 853) They were immensely relieved when the decision was taken not to allow school boards to influence the amount of financial support made available for church schools; but there remained some division of opinion among them about the desirability of becoming members of boards, though Cardinal Manning's influence in favour of this was decisive.[2]

It may be noted here that the government's favourable attitude towards the voluntary bodies was made very clear when its policy in relation to training colleges was announced. The existing system was disadvantageous to Nonconformists. The Voluntaryists had spurned government building grants when these had been available (up to 1862): the result was that they now were much less well provided with colleges than were the Anglicans and Roman Catholics—and therefore less able to take advantage of the generous annual grants now paid by the state. The Act had made no reference to training colleges, and the government indicated in 1871 that there would be no question of establishing colleges having a position corresponding to that of board schools. The colleges would continue to be free to admit students without any restrictions laid down by the Education Department other than those concerned with age and suitability for the profession.[3]

Many Nonconformists were bitterly resentful of their 'betrayal' by their own Liberal party, and the National Education League remained in being to promote the formation of school boards wherever possible, to resist any increase of grants to denominational schools, and to campaign for a national system of elementary education that would be free, compulsory and unsectarian. In 1872 the League decided to campaign for the election in all districts of school boards which would control the secular education in all aided elementary schools, including voluntary schools; moreover it at last adopted the 'secularist' policy and demanded that in schools established by school boards religious instruction, if desired, should be the concern of the different denominations, and be given outside the normal curriculum by their own teachers and without expense to the board. In 1870 the Central Nonconformist Committee began to agitate for the refusal of government aid to new denominational schools and its gradual withdrawal from existing ones[4]. Even many Wesleyans now favoured this policy, and still more wished to see the universal establishment of school boards.[5]

But the great weakness of the Nonconformist position, as always, was indecision about religious instruction. Gladstone wrote to John Bright: 'the noncons. have not yet as a body made up their minds whether they want unsectarian religion, or whether they want simple secular teaching, so far as the application of the rate is concerned.' He himself would 'never be a party' to the former; the Liberal party could only decline to give definite pledges and 'adjourn for a while the solution of the grave parts of the education problem.'[6] The resentment of the Nonconformists helped in 1874 to change a Liberal majority of 110 into a Conservative one of 66. This hardly favoured their cause; but hard facts were becoming more obviously important than political and religious affiliations, and the new Conservative government had far less freedom of action than its supporters had hoped.

2 Competition in School Supply

Since feelings ran so high in many parts of the country, the voluntary bodies naturally wished to establish as many schools as possible whilst grants in aid of building were still available. Conscientious objection to the limited religious instruction available in board schools was often reinforced not only by partisan rivalry but also by the desire of many ratepayers to avoid paying rates to a school board. The applications for building grants each year had hitherto normally numbered about 150[7]; but now, in the period of less than five months between the passing of the Act and the final date for receipt of applications (31 December 1870), there were 3342 applications, in respect of which 1633 grants were made towards the provision of over 280,000 school places, at a cost to the voluntary subscribers of more than £1,348,000[8]. The last grant was paid in 1881, but, even so, voluntary provision continued to increase at a surprising rate for some years.

In many districts efforts to avoid the establishment of a school board were successful. In many others school board elections became extensions of existing political and religious conflicts,[9] and the cumulative system of voting (since it facilitated the representation even of small minorities and encouraged the making of electoral compacts), stimulated this. The result was that school boards were often controlled by those who favoured the voluntary system and who were unwilling to encourage what they considered unfair competition from board schools.[10] The school boards in rural areas were frequently particularly inactive and inefficient. On the other hand, whether as the result of genuine enthusiasm for the spread of education, or of political or religious hostility to the voluntary system, or of the pressure of public opinion, many very active boards were soon set up. The London board was particularly energetic and resourceful.

The Act, as we noted, had given vague or even contradictory guidance regarding the authorisation of new building where, in the course of time, additional schools became 'necessary'. Indeed there was no guidance at all relating to areas where no school board existed, though in 1878 a minute of the Committee of Council ruled that 'a school situated in a district which is not under a school board shall not be deemed to be unnecessary if it has, for the previous twelve months, been recognised by the Department as a "certified efficient school," and has had, during that period, an average attendance of not less than 30 scholars.'[11] (By an oddity of legal drafting, section 98 of the Act conferred no right on the Department to refuse grant to an *enlarged* school, whether the extension was considered 'unnecessary' or not).[12]

Within school board districts difficulties arose. Section 98 empowered the Education Department to refuse a grant to a school not already in receipt of one 'if they think the school is unnecessary,' but the use of the word 'may' seemed to imply some freedom of action. This the Department was unwilling to exercise; and by a minute agreed in 1876 and embodied in the Code in 1878, it even divested itself for a few years of any freedom in the matter. In practice decisions as to 'necessity' (and therefore of entitlement to annual grants) were left to the local school boards. 'Necessity' having been established, it was contended that the prior right to make good the deficiency was, by section 18, vested in the school board—and the law officers of the Crown even ruled that the board could not divest itself of this duty.[13] Of course one factor making a new school 'necessary' would be 'suitability' on religious grounds, but this was not defined in the Act; and it was often argued that since a Church of England school in a single-school area was considered to become 'suitable' for Nonconformist children because of the operation of the conscience clause, then the children of Anglicans and Roman Catholics, similarly protected by the clause, might be expected to attend board schools.

As decisions were left to school boards there were some notorious disputes when they were inflexible or prejudiced (one case involving a Roman Catholic school in a Swansea suburb aroused particularly heated controversy); but the publicity given to these conflicts indicated that they were relatively few. The great majority of boards showed more tolerance (the London board 'never refused their consent to new voluntary schools being put upon the annual grant list, however well supplied with schools the district might already be');[14] and some boards welcomed the establishment of voluntary schools as resulting in a saving of rates. The Education Department was in general sympathetic; the representation of minorities on school boards afforded some protection; and by 1888 even the Nonconformist members of the Cross Commission set up to investigate the working of the Act were recommending 'a more liberal interpretation of the word "suitability".'[15]

3 The Religious Settlement

Forster had confidently predicted that although the fate of the Bill would depend upon the actual words used in regard to the 'religious difficulty', most school boards would in practice prescribe unsectarian religious instruction; but even he must have been surprised to see what little influence the parliamentary debates and resolutions on this vexed question had upon the decisions ultimately taken by the vast majority of school boards. The London School Board, whose example was at once widely copied, ordered that 'the Cowper-Temple clause be strictly observed,' but added that this must be done 'both in letter and spirit,' which it took to imply 'that no attempt be made to attach children to any denomination.'[16] It thus blandly acted as if Jacob Bright's amendment had been passed instead of being decisively rejected. (And indeed many school boards also adopted his proposed prohibition of attempts to 'detach' children from any denomination).[17] The government's careful and explicit interpretation of the Cowper-Temple clause was almost everywhere ignored or defied.

Sometimes, perhaps, there was genuine misunderstanding of the clause, but (since the heated debates could scarcely have failed to attract attention) this could not have been common. The fact was that a school board of very mixed membership could hardly permit teachers of various persuasions to expound different, contradictory, even highly controversial religious views within the same school—whatever Gladstone had said about religious freedom. The teachers showed no inclination to resent the loss of such freedom; the board schools were (generally speaking) outside the control of clerical disputants; and practical considerations now demanded quick decisions, not prolonged discussions on matters of principle. Parents (apart from exceptions already noted) cared little about doctrinal differences. The result was that the 'non-sectarian' solution of one kind or other was widely accepted, and this so quickly that considerable surprise was evinced when, in 1887, the Manchester School Board was found to be providing denominational instruction in its schools—quite legally, as the Education Department admitted.[18]

Relatively few boards took advantage of the right to provide only secular instruction, and most of these were in Wales,[19] where Nonconformist feeling was strong and the principle that religious instruction should be left to home and chapel was both firmly believed in and acted upon. When the Liberals, Nonconformists and Radicals obtained control of the school board in Birmingham (the home of the National Education League) in 1873, they attempted to enforce the League's policy in board schools by permitting religious instruction to be given only after school hours and then not by the school's teachers. The system failed because of divisions of opinion about the policy among the Nonconformists, the opposition of Anglicans, and the incompetence of the inexperienced instructors. Its failure in the very capital of the League was widely taken to have demonstrated decisively that the 'secular solution' was impracticable and generally unacceptable.

Henceforward the Nonconformists tended to concentrate on demands for greater facilities for training their teachers, and on allegations of unfair treatment arising from breaches of the conscience clause and of the rule preventing the use of catechisms and distinctive formularies in board schools. There were disputes, involving Gladstone himself, as to whether the Apostle's Creed was such a formulary:[20] despite his favourable verdict its teaching was eventually forbidden by most school boards.[21] For a time the Liverpool School Board ruled that the Roman Catholic version of the Bible was a distinctive formulary.[22] It was particularly difficult to give 'neutral' religious instruction without incurring criticism from Unitarians, who were politically very active within the Education League and elsewhere. Yet the work of the board schools went on, with such disputes causing minimal disturbance.

4 The Financial Framework

For more than thirty years after the passage of the Act the essential conflict of views and principles found expression above all in battles over finance. The government had obtained legal sanction for a policy which Gladstone had optimistically summarised in the words:

> I think . . . we may fairly require the promoters of voluntary schools to supply from their own resources and the pence of the children, what, with the grant from the Exchequer, will enable them to perfectly well stand in competition with the rated schools. (H., CCII, 282)

This was vague, but the Act was in some respects even vaguer, and the contestants felt obliged, even before the main battles could commence, to straighten out several salients.

A The Remission of School Fees

Section 25 of the Act empowered a school board, 'if they think fit,' to pay part or all of the fees of necessitous children; no such payment might be 'made or refused on condition of the child attending any public elementary school other than such as may be selected by the parent.' This remission of fees and this safeguard were clearly particularly necessary where school boards made use of their powers to make attendance compulsory. But it involved the principle of rate support for denominational schools, and aroused the most acrimonious controversy. The Birmingham town council (dominated by opponents of the voluntary system) refused for almost three years, in spite of insistent legal rulings, to levy a rate to pay fees to denominational schools when required to do so by the first local school board (controlled from 1870-3 by supporters of voluntary schools).[23] The Manchester and Salford authorities were more generous, or, as opponents declared, less scrupulous. The sums involved were remarkably small. As John Morley, Gladstone's Nonconformist biographer, admitted in a passionate attack on the section, 'the total amount contributed to the support of denominational schools . . . in the year 1872 was no more than the trifling sum of £5,070 . . . and of this . . . no less than £3,405 were paid in Manchester and Salford alone.' Yet, he went on, though it was a small matter 'so were Hampden's twenty shillings.'[24] In the general election of 1874, of the 425 Liberal candidates in Great Britain, 300 were pledged to demand the repeal of this detested section;[25] but it was in fact repealed in 1876 by a Conservative government which substituted the provision that the payments on behalf of indigent children should be made by Poor Law Guardians.

B Voluntary Contributions

As we have remarked, Gladstone had given an undertaking that voluntary contributions would be required in respect of denominational schools, and he had implied that these might fairly represent about one-sixth of annual costs, but Forster had spoken against such a requirement, which in fact did not form part of the Act. Critics were quick to point out the consequences, in some areas, of this omission. Thus from figures given by John Morley (admittedly selective) it can be calculated that for seven schools in the Manchester and Salford area in 1870-1 the voluntary contributions averaged only about 5.8 per cent of total expenditure.[26] In Stockport in 1884-5 the parents provided 47.7 per cent of the income, the taxpayers 48.8 per cent and subscribers only 3.5 per cent; the chairman of the school attendance committee explained: 'We generally expect that the schools shall be self-supporting, with the Government grant and the children's fees.'[27] Such cases were exceptional, however; indeed in 1880 and 1890, over the whole of Britain, the average annual income from voluntary contributions was apparently of the order of 21 and 18 per cent respectively (and this does not take into account the cost of new schools or structural alterations).[28] But there were very wide variations,[29] and the practice in some places of charging relatively high fees (sometimes to discourage the attendance of 'unsatisfactory' children)[30] tended there to defeat the main intentions of the Act.

C The Government Grant

As we have seen, the implication of Gladstone's promise when building grants were withdrawn was that the state would increase its grant by 50 per cent; this would have involved raising its average annual contribution to one-half of the average annual expenditure, or (on the figures he supplied for existing voluntary schools) to 15s (75p) for each child attending. In fact the average government grant to voluntary schools did not reach this amount until 1878. Steps to improve the situation were taken in 1876: special assistance was given for particularly ill-provided schools in scattered areas, and, more generally, it was decided that payment of government grant up to 17/6 (87½p) would not depend upon an equal sum being forthcoming from local sources, though this condition would operate for grant payments above that level. The figure was chosen as representing half the average annual cost 'per scholar in attendance', but in fact the state grant did not quite amount to half the actual annual expenditure until after 1891, when, as we shall see, the government assumed responsibility for providing a large proportion of the income formerly derived from school fees. But, once again, it must be emphasised that no account is here taken of the cost of new schools or of structural alterations to existing schools—none of this expenditure being met from government sources after 1881.

D   School Fees

The financial basis of the Act had included the assumption that school fees would, on average, amount to about one-third of the annual expenditure. But of course parental ability and willingness to provide school pence varied widely: the Wesleyan schools (by no means always attended by Wesleyan children) could, and usually did, charge much higher fees than the Roman Catholic. In 1885-6 the annual income obtained from school fees 'per scholar in average attendance' in the various voluntary schools was as follows: Wesleyan, 16s 1d (80p); British and Undenominational, 13s 7¾d (68p); Church of England, 10s 8d (53p); and Roman Catholic, 9s 5½d (47p). There were wide variations in board schools also, depending on the local willingness to spend rates: in Manchester the average school pence amounted to 15s 4¼d (77p), in Birmingham to only 6s 4½d (32p).[31]

The requirement that parents should pay fees, though in accord with hallowed beliefs and convenient also on grounds of economy, obviously meant that the quality of education provided depended on the ability and willingness of parents to pay, and was likely to suffer where low fees had to be charged, especially as in those areas voluntary subscriptions were also often low. Moreover, since government grants to some extent depended on the income from other sources, the situation was perpetuated which had so often been deplored (notably, as we have seen, by the Newcastle Commission and by Forster himself when introducing his Bill) whereby least help was available where it was most needed.

The system made it particularly difficult to demand and enforce compulsory attendance. In 1876 the Conservatives introduced a system of indirect compulsion: no child under ten was to be employed nor one between ten and fourteeen unless he had reached a certain proficiency in the three R's, or at least made a prescribed number of school attendances. School attendance committees were established to enforce the system in districts which had no school board, and it was declared to be the duty of the parent to 'cause his child to receive efficient elementary instruction' in the three Rs. In 1880 the Liberals went further by requiring school boards and school attendance committees to insist upon school attendance between the ages of ten and thirteen, unless a certificate of proficiency was forthcoming. Naturally one result of this legislation was to increase the need for school places and to create difficulties with needy or negligent parents. In 1891 a Conservative government passed the 'Free Schooling' Elementary Education Act, which provided state grants to make possible either the abolition of school fees where these had been up to ten shillings (50p) per annum, or the reduction by that amount where they had been greater. Even more important, the Act ensured that parents might demand free education for their children. It thus became possible to extend the range of compulsory attendance: in 1893 the earliest age at which a child might be completely or partially excused from attendance was raised to eleven, in 1899 (except in agricultural districts) to twelve. In 1900 local authorities were empowered to raise the age of compulsory attendance to fourteen.

E   Rates

Both Gladstone and Forster had thought it unlikely that the ratepayers would ever be called upon to pay to school boards more than 3d in the £; but in England by 1884 only 26.6 per cent

of the school boards in boroughs and 11.5 per cent of those in
parishes were spending rates of under 3d; 38.2 per cent of the
boards in boroughs and 52.4 per cent of those in parishes were
spending more than twice this amount and some more than four
times as much.[32]

F 'Unfair Competition'

Compulsory attendance and constantly rising standards
naturally led to increased expenditure. The more active and conscientious school boards were anxious to provide good buildings,
equipment and teachers, and to extend the curriculum. This extension would surely have been necessary in any case because of
the extremely wide range of ability among the children. Since
existing facilities for secondary education were very limited, and,
in general, rarely available for working-class children, there was
considerable pressure on the elementary schools to provide more
than elementary education. This the Act clearly permitted, and
the system of 'payment by results' was gradually made more
flexible to allow for it (though the system was not finally
abolished until 1897). Progressive boards set up higher grade elementary schools or higher classes in ordinary elementary schools;
state grants were made available for organised science classes in
both types of elementary school; rate-aided evening elementary
schools began instructing adult students.

All this made it more difficult for the voluntary schools to 'per-
fectly well stand in competition,' as Gladstone had put it, with
the board schools. In 1872 the annual 'average cost per child in
average attendance' had been roughly equal in the two types of
school: £1 7s 5d (£1.37) in voluntary schools, £1 8s 4$\frac{1}{4}$d (£1.42)
in board schools; but by 1895-6 the figure for voluntary schools
was £1 18s 11$\frac{1}{4}$d (£1.95), whilst that for board schools was 28.7
per cent higher at £2 10s 1$\frac{3}{4}$d (£2.51). The difference arose not so
much because the board schools qualified for higher government
grants—for years the difference had been only a shilling (5p) or
less; and by this time the question of fees was not important. But
the amount provided for voluntary schools by contributions was
6s 9d (34p), that for board schools from rates was 19s 8d (98p).
Moreover, these figures take no account of the cost of building
and structural repairs, where the board schools had the enormous
advantages of being able to spend far more, to borrow money on

the security of the rates, and to acquire sites by compulsory purchase. And more money was available to them for teachers'
salaries: in 1895 average salaries were in general 32 per cent
higher in board schools than in aided voluntary schools; in London they were about 65 per cent higher, and in Birmingham,
Manchester and Liverpool about 50 per cent higher.[33]

It is remarkable that, in spite of its handicaps, the voluntary
system continued to expand. By 1895 roughly four out of every
seven children in average attendance in grant-aided elementary
schools were still in voluntary schools; but since 1876 the numbers in the latter had increased only by about 48 per cent,
whereas the percentage increase in board schools had been about
ten times this figure.[34] Moreover, most of the voluntary schools, of
course, were older and smaller (the average accommodation
being about 250 as against about 440 in board schools); and
whereas the attendance rate in voluntary schools was about two-
thirds, it was about four-fifths in board schools.[35]

In the face of this situation various reactions were possible.
The voluntary bodies naturally complained that the boards were
spending too much public money and attempting too much.
Thus Thomas Allies, the secretary of the Catholic Poor School
Committee, protested that the board schools were giving 'an education which does not properly belong to the children of the
parents in their actual condition';[36] those members of the Cross
Commission favourable to the voluntary schools objected to the
teaching in board schools of 'languages, classical and modern,
and advanced science', and complained that 'not a few children
of the wealthier classes' were attending these schools. They suggested that 'the instruction to be paid out of the rates and taxes
should be fixed by the Legislature.'[37] Probably much more important was the influence on the policies of individual school
boards of those members who objected to what they considered
unfair competition with voluntary schools, or, more simply, to
increases in rates.

A more positive proposal for dealing with the situation came
from those who asked for rate support for voluntary schools.
Since both sides in the conflict were by 1890 reconciled to each
other's continued existence in the educational field,[38] an amicable
agreement might have seemed possible, especially as the voluntary contributions and school fees now formed such a small pro-

portion of annual income (though the former had still to be relied on for new building). But would not rate-aid lead to public
control and insistence on the Cowper-Temple clause as now
generally interpreted? The voluntary bodies were divided about
the wisdom of claiming rate aid: the Archbishop of Canterbury
was against, Cardinal Manning in favour—but even he was
opposed by the secretary of the Catholic Poor School Committee.[39] The majority report of the Cross Commission, representing the views of those favourable to voluntary schools,
suggested a compromise: rate support to equal voluntary subscriptions, with a maximum of 10s (50p).[40] But the opposition was
formidable; and in 1899 the Education Department demonstrated
vividly the crumbling financial foundations of the Act when it
somewhat querulously pointed out that voluntary contributions
might well be kept up if more use were made of 'collections,
bazaars, entertainments and the like.'[41]

5 Administration

The administrative problems created by the Act were many,
and it is possible to indicate only a few of them briefly here.
(i) The system by which school boards, though not themselves
empowered to levy a rate, could require local government bodies
to do so, led to constant friction between the two: this was best
exemplified by the struggle (already referred to) between the
school board and the town council in Birmingham in 1870-3 over
the operation of section 25. (ii) There was still inadequate control of the supply and quality of education, for voluntary schools
were often ill-housed, some voluntary managers and school
boards apathetic, the Education Department remote from the
local scene. (iii) The 'dual system' did not create two distinct
fields of action engaged in fruitful competition, for supporters
of voluntary schools frequently considered it part of their duty,
as such, to seek membership of school boards (even to endeavour
to 'capture' them) with a view to limiting their activities where
these were considered unduly expensive or otherwise 'unfair' to
the voluntary schools. (iv) By 1902 there were more than 2,500
school boards and more than 20,000 voluntary schools; and each
board and the managers of each voluntary school had the right

of direct access to the Education Department. The result was a situation in the central administration constantly verging on chaos, with long delays and much haphazard procedure.[42]

6 Conclusion

Before the end of the nineteenth century it was clear that a new Education Act was urgently needed to deal with the difficulties we have described. But it is perhaps necessary to remind ourselves that, in spite of the problems which it failed to solve, and others to which it gave rise, the passing of the Elementary Education Act of 1870 was one of the most important events in Britain's history. By the end of the century it had laid the firm foundations of a national system of elementary education, and had even made it possible to envisage the establishment of a similar system of secondary education. True, the Act had to be modified and reinforced in the decades following 1870 by more generous provisions encouraging free schooling, compulsory attendance and the development of voluntary and board schools alike; but it had acknowledged the ultimate responsibility of the government for the education of the people; it had made it possible for those of very different views to obtain or supply education in ways generally in accordance with their principles and consciences; and it had helped to establish the status of teachers as men and women who might well feel disposed to co-operate with the clergy, but who were free to insist upon the dignity, value and independence of their own professional commitments.

Perhaps the greatest virtue of the Act (as making future progress possible) was that, as Forster had predicted, it enabled a solution to be found to the problem of providing a generally acceptable form of religious instruction for schools wholly supplied and maintained from public funds. The solution, as we have noted, was not the one decided upon by parliament; but this is a happy reminder of one great advantage of parliamentary government—that its decisions, when they run counter to public opinion, can (sometimes) easily be ignored.

(Notes to this section are on pages 82-3)

NOTES

Section One (pp 8-34)

1 Central Society of Education, *First Publication* (1837), I, 161
2 These included such very different figures as J. A. Roebuck and Sir James Kay-Shuttleworth, first secretary to the Committee of Council on Education
3 For more detailed modern studies of the 'religious difficulty' in the period prior to 1870 *see* the author's *The Religious Problem in English Education: The Crucial Experiment,* and *Church, State and Schools in Britain*
4 *Report of the Select Committee on the Education of the Poorer Classes (1838),* Q.524
5 Binns, *A Century of Education . . . ,* 113
6 *See* Akenside, *The Irish Experiment . . .*
7 *See* Murphy, *The Religious Problem in English Education . . .*
8 *Four Periods of Public Education,* 40
9 *Minutes of the Committee of Council, 1839-40,* viii (referred to henceforward as *MCC*)
10 Ibid, 24
11 Diamond, *Work of Catholic Poor School Committee . . . ,* 48
12 Rigg, *National Education,* 145
13 Denison, *Notes of My Life,* 136-40
14 *MCC, 1853-4,* I, 65
15 *Report of Committee of Council, 1859-60,* xxxi (referred to henceforward as *RCC*)
16 *RCC, 1861-2,* xxiv
17 *See* Simon, *Studies in the History of Education, 1780-1870,* 361-4
18 Hansard, *Parliamentary Debates,* CLXXVIII, 1549
19 Baines, *National Education . . . ,* 3-8
20 *RCC, 1869-70,* Table 2
21 *Report,* I, 316
22 *Return, Confined to the Municipal Boroughs of Birmingham, Leeds, Liverpool and Manchester . . . ,* 174
23 Of the government grant for the year 1868-9 (excluding costs of administration) 74.5 per cent was paid in respect of

Church of England schools, 13.7 per cent for schools attached
to the British Society, 6.1 per cent for Wesleyan schools, and
5.1 per cent for Roman Catholic schools. (Calculated from
statistics in *RCC, 1869-70*, lxxviii)

24 *See* Burgess, *Enterprise in Education*, 195
25 The fullest evidence on parental attitudes towards religious
    instruction about 1860 is given in the report of the New-
    castle Commission, summarised in vol. 1, pp 34-9. *See
    also* the author's *Church, State and Schools in Britain . . . ,*
    pp 7-9
26 Vol I, 39

Section Two (pp 35-64)

1 *Return, Confined to the Municipal Boroughs of Birmingham, Leeds, Liverpool and Manchester, of Schools for the
   Poorer Classes* . . . The figures quoted are actually rough
   approximations to those given in the report
2 *RCC, 1869-70*, xxvi
3 *See* letter quoted by Selby, *British Journal of Educational
   Studies*, XVIII, No 2, 200
4 *See Return, Confined to the Municipal Boroughs of Birmingham, Leeds, etc, of Schools for the Poorer Classes . . . ,*
   170
5 Calculated from *RCC, 1869-70*, Table 7
6 *RCC, 1869-70*, xxvi. Detailed guidance was provided; thus,
   'simple policemen, coast guards and dock and railway porters
   may commonly be regarded as labouring men. But petty
   officers in these services . . . and clerks of various kinds present more difficulty.' Among questions which might help to
   resolve the problem were, 'Does he rank and associate with
   the working men or with the tradesmen of the place?' (ibid,
   lxi)
7 Forster was evidently quoting the figure for average annual
   expenditure given in *RCC, 1869-70*, Table 2
8 Rigg, *National Education*, 367-8
9 *RCC, 1881-2*, xi
10 Rigg, *National Education*, 365-6
11 *MCC, 1853-4*, 45

F

12 *RCC, 1869-70,* xxvi
13 Morley, *Life of W. E. Gladstone,* II, 306
14 *Correspondence,* ed Lathbury, II, 137-8
15 Ibid, II, 8
16 Tropp, *The School Teachers,* 105
17 Quoted Armytage, *A. J. Mundella,* 220

Section Three (pp 65-79)

1 For accounts of the policies and actions of the different religious and political groups at this time *see,* in particular, Cruickshank, *Church and State in English Education,* and Murphy, *Church, State and Schools in Britain, 1800-1970;* for a fuller but less impartial version *see also* Adams, *History of the Elementary School Contest in England*
2 *See* Selby, 'Henry Edward Manning and the Education Bill of 1870,' *British Journal of Educational Studies,* XVIII, No 2
3 *RCC, 1870-1,* cxvi
4 Adams, *History of the Elementary School Contest in England,* 239
5 Cross Commission, *Third Report,* 51
6 Morley, *Life of W. E. Gladstone,* II, 311
7 Morley, *The Struggle for National Education,* 17
8 *RCC, 1885-6,* xi
9 *See* Richards, 'Religious Controversy and the School Boards,' *British Journal of Educational Studies,* XVIII, No 2
10 *See,* e g Cross Commission, Final Report, 358-9
11 *RCC, 1877-8,* 330. There was a restriction based on the size of population if another school was available
12 Cross Commission, *First Report,* 26
13 Cross Commission, *Final Report,* 56
14 Ibid, 57
15 Ibid, 241
16 Spalding, *The Work of the London School Board,* 99
17 *See* Murphy, *Church, State and Schools in Britain* . . . , 68, and relevant returns listed in bibliography below
18 Cross Commission, *Second Report,* 785-6
19 *See* Murphy, *Church, State and Schools in Britain* . . . , 69
20 Ibid, 66-7

21 Gregory, *Elementary Education*, 130
22 Midwinter, E., *Old Liverpool*, 121
23 *See* Taylor, *Birmingham and the Movement for National Education*
24 *The Struggle for National Education*, 8-9
25 *Life of W. E. Gladstone*, II, 311
26 *The Struggle for National Education*, 52
27 Cross Commission, *Final Report*, 266 (The percentages have been re-calculated from the figures given, since the commissioners clearly confused income and expenditure)
28 Calculated from statistics in *RCC, 1895-6*, Table E
29 The average annual voluntary contribution in 1886 was, in Brighton, nearly 11/8 (58p), in London nearly 8/10 (44p) and in Liverpool 2/10 (14p) *RCC, 1885-6*, x
30 Cross Commission, *Final Report*, 267
31 *RCC, 1885-6*, x
32 Ibid, xxxv
33 Calculated from returns in *RCC, 1895-6*, Table G (The figures are based on salary expenditure 'per scholar in average attendance')
34 Calculated from returns in ibid, Table F
35 Calculated from returns in ibid, Table F
36 Cross Commission, *Final Report*, 370
37 Ibid, 145-6
38 *See* Murphy, *Church, State and Schools in Britain*, 71
39 Cross Commission, *Final Report*, 355
40 Ibid, 222
41 Beales, 'The Struggle for the Schools', in *The English Catholics 1850-1950*, 383
42 *See* Kekewich, *The Education Department and After*

SECTION FOUR

TEXT OF THE ELEMENTARY EDUCATION ACT, 1870

(33 & 34 Vict. c 75)

[Note: some sections and paragraphs have been omitted as dealing with regulations (such as those relating to the use of casting votes, the production of receipts for auditors, and similar rules) which it was necessary for the Act to prescribe, but which add nothing to its significance for a modern reader. Asterisks indicate where omissions occur. One section of the Act (20) has been briefly paraphrased, since it was expressed largely in terms of references to other Acts, and would convey little meaning without extensive quotations from them.]

An Act to provide for public Elementary Education in England and Wales.

BE it enacted by the Queen's most Excellent Majesty, by and with the advice and consent of the Lords Spiritual and Temporal, and Commons, in this present Parliament assembled, and by the authority of the same, as follows; (that is to say,)

Preliminary

Short title

1. This Act may be cited as "The Elementary Education Act, 1870."

Extent of Act.
Definition of terms.

2. This Act shall not extend to Scotland or Ireland.

3. In this Act—

     *   *   *   *   *

The term "Education Department" means "the Lords of the Committee of the Privy Council on Education:"

The term "Her Majesty's inspectors" means the inspectors of schools appointed by Her Majesty on the recommendation of the Education Department:

The term "managers" includes all persons who have the management of any elementary school, whether the legal interest in the schoolhouse is or is not vested in them:

     *   *   *   *   *

The term "elementary school" means a school or department of a school at which elementary education is the principal part of the education there given, and does not include any school or department of a school at which the ordinary payments in respect of the instruction, from each scholar, exceed ninepence a week:

The term "schoolhouse" includes the teacher's dwelling house, and the playground (if any) and the offices and all premises belonging to or required for a school:

The term "vestry" means the ratepayers of a parish meeting in vestry according to law:

The term "ratepayer" includes every person who, under the provisions of the Poor Rate Assessment and Collection Act, 1869, is deemed to be duly rated:

The term "parliamentary grant" means a grant made in aid of an elementary school, either annually or otherwise, out of moneys provided by Parliament for the civil service, intituled 'For public education in Great Britain.'

(I) Local Provision for Schools

★   ★   ★   ★   ★

Supply of Schools

5. There shall be provided for every school district a sufficient amount of accommodation in public elementary schools (as hereinafter defined) available for all the children resident in such district for whose elementary education efficient and suitable provision is not otherwise made, and where there is an insufficient amount of such accommodation, in this Act referred to as "public school accommodation," the deficiency shall be supplied in manner provided by this Act.

School district to have sufficient public schools.

6. Where the Education Department, in the manner provided by this Act, are satisfied and have given public notice that there is an insufficient amount of public school accommodation for any school district, and the deficiency is not supplied as herein-after required, a school board shall be formed for such district and shall supply such deficiency, and in case of default by the school board the Education Department shall cause the duty of such board to be performed in manner provided by this Act.

Supply of schools in case of deficiency.

7. Every elementary school which is conducted in accordance with the following regulations shall be a public elementary school within the meaning of this Act; and every public elementary school shall be conducted in accordance with the following regulations (a copy of which regulations shall be conspicuously put up in every such school); namely,

Regulations for conduct of public elementary school.

(1.) It shall not be required, as a condition of any child being admitted into or continuing in the school, that he shall attend or abstain from attending any Sunday school, or any place of religious worship, or that he shall attend any religious observance or any instruction in religious subjects in the school or elsewhere, from which observance or instruction he may be withdrawn by his parent, or that he shall, if withdrawn by his parent, attend the school on any day exclusively set apart for religious observance by the religious body to which his parent belongs:

(2.) The time or times during which any religious observance is practised or instruction in religious subjects is given at any meeting of the school shall be either at the beginning or at the end or at the beginning and the end of such meeting, and shall be inserted in a time table to be approved by the Education Department, and to be kept permanently and conspicuously affixed in every schoolroom; and any scholar may be withdrawn by his parent from such observance or instruction without forfeiting any of the other benefits of the school:

(3.) The school shall be open at all times to the inspection of any of Her Majesty's inspectors, so, however, that it shall be no part of the duties of such inspector to inquire into any instruction in religious subjects given at such school, or to examine any scholar therein in religious knowledge or in any religious subject or book.

(4.) The school shall be conducted in accordance with the conditions required to be fulfilled by an elementary school in order to obtain an annual parliamentary grant.

Proceedings for Supply of Schools

Determination by Education Department of deficiency of public school accommodation

8. For the purpose of determining with respect to every school district the amount of public school accommodation, if any, required for such district, the Education Department shall, immediately after the passing of this Act, cause such returns to be made as in this Act mentioned, and on receiving those returns, and after such inquiry, if any, as they think necessary, shall consider whether any and what public school accommodation is

required for such district, and in so doing they shall take into consideration every school, whether public elementary or not, and whether actually situated in the school district or not, which in their opinion gives, or will when completed give, efficient elementary education to, and is, or will when completed be, suitable for the children of such district.

9. The Education Department shall publish a notice of their decision as to the public school accommodation for any school district, setting forth with respect to such district the description thereof, the number, size, and description of the schools (if any) available for such district, which the Education Department have taken into consideration as above mentioned, and the amount and description of the public school accommodation, if any, which appears to them to be required for the district, and any other particulars which the Education Department think expedient.

Notice by Education Department of public school accommodation required

If any persons being either—

(1.) Ratepayers of the district, not less than ten, or if less than ten being rated to the poor rate upon a rateable value of not less than one third of the whole rateable value of the district, or,

(2.) The managers of any elementary school in the district,

feel aggrieved by such decision, such persons may, within one month after the publication of the notice, apply in writing to the Education Department for and the Education Department shall direct the holding of a public inquiry in manner provided by this Act.

At any time after the expiration of such month, if no public inquiry is directed, or after the receipt of the report made after such inquiry, as the case may be, the Education Department may, if they think that the amount of public school accommodation for the district is insufficient, publish a final notice stating the same particulars as were contained in the former notice, with such modifications (if any) as they think fit to make, and directing that the public school accommodation therein mentioned as required be supplied.

Formation of school board and requisition to provide schools.

10. If after the expiration of a time, not exceeding six months, to be limited by the final notice, the Education Department are satisfied that all the public school accommodation required by the final notice to be supplied has not been so supplied, nor is in course of being supplied with due despatch, the Education Department shall cause a school board to be formed for the district as provided in this Act, and shall send a requisition to the school board so formed requiring them to take proceedings forthwith for supplying the public school accommodation mentioned in the requisition, and the school board shall supply the same accordingly.

Proceedings on default of school board.

11. If the school board fail to comply with the requisition within twelve months after the sending of such requisition in manner aforesaid, they shall be deemed to be in default, and if the Education Department are satisfied that such board are in default they may proceed in manner directed by this Act with respect to a school board in default.

12. In the following cases, (that is to say,)

Formation of school board. Formation of school boards without inquiry upon application.

(1.) Where application is made to the Education Department with respect to any school district by the persons who, if there were a school board in that district, would elect the school board, or with respect to any borough, by the council;

(2.) Where the Education Department are satisfied that the managers of any elementary school in any school district are unable or unwilling any longer to maintain such school, and that if the school is discontinued the amount of public school accommodation for such district will be insufficient,

the Education Department may, if they think fit, without making the inquiry or publishing the notices required by this Act before the formation of a school board, but after such inquiry public or other, and such notice as the Education Department think sufficient, cause a school board to be formed for such district, and send a requisition to such school board in the same manner in all respects as if they had published a final notice.

An application for the purposes of this section may be made by a resolution passed by the said electing body after notice published at least a week previously, or by the Council, and the provisions of the second part of the second schedule to this Act with respect to the passing of such resolution shall be observed.

13. After the receipt of any returns under this Act sub- *Proceedings* sequently to the first with respect to any school district, *by Educa-* and after such inquiry as the Education Department *tion De-* think necessary, the Education Department shall consider *partment* whether any and what public school accommodation is *after the* required in such district in the same manner as in the case *first year* of the first returns under this Act, and where in such district there is no school board acting under this Act they may issue notices and take proceedings in the same manner as they may after the receipt of the first returns under this Act, and where there is a school board in such district they shall proceed in manner directed by this Act.

Management and Maintenance of Schools by School Board

14. Every school provided by a school board shall be *Manage-* conducted under the control and management of such *ment of* board in accordance with the following regulations: *school*
by school
  (1.) The school shall be a public elementary school *board.*
      within the meaning of this Act:
  (2.) No religious catechism or religious formulary
      which is distinctive of any particular denomination shall be taught in the school.

15. The school board may, if they think fit, from time *Appoint-* to time delegate any of their powers under this Act ex- *ment of* cept the power of raising money, and in particular may *managers* delegate the control and management of any school pro- *by school* vided by them, with or without any conditions or re- *board.* strictions, to a body of managers appointed by them, consisting of not less than three persons.

The school board may from time to time remove all or any of such managers and within the limits allowed by this section add to or diminish the number of or otherwise alter the constitution or powers of any body of managers by it under this section.

$$\star \quad \star \quad \star \quad \star \quad \star$$

Neglect by board of regulations of public elementary schools.

16. If the school board do or permit any act in contravention of or fail to comply with the regulations according to which a school provided by them is required by this Act to be conducted, the Education Department may declare the school board to be and such board shall accordingly be deemed to be a board in default, and the Education Department may proceed accordingly, and every act or omission of any member of the school board, or manager appointed by them, or any person under the control of the board, shall be deemed to be permitted by the board, unless the contrary be proved.

If any dispute arises as to whether the school board have done or permitted any act in contravention of or have failed to comply with the said regulations, the matter shall be referred to the Education Department, whose decision thereon shall be final.

Fees of children.

17. Every child attending a school provided by any school board shall pay such weekly fee as may be prescribed by the school board, with the consent of the Education Department, but the school board may from time to time, for a renewable period not exceeding six months, remit the whole or any part of such fee in the case of any child when they are of opinion that the parent of such child is unable from poverty to pay the same, but such remission shall not be deemed to be parochial relief given to such parent.

Maintenance by school board of schools and sufficient school accommodation

18. The school board shall maintain and keep efficient every school provided by such board, and shall from time to time provide such additional school accommodation as is, in their opinion, necessary in order to supply a sufficient amount of public school accommodation for their district.

A school board may discontinue any school provided by them, or change the site of any such school, if they satisfy the Education Department that the school to be discontinued is unnecessary, or that such change of site is expedient.

If at any time the Education Department are satisfied that a school board have failed to perform their duty, either by not maintaining or keeping efficient every school provided by them, or by not providing such additional school accommodation as in the opinion of the Education Department is necessary in order to supply a sufficient amount of public school accommodation in their district, the Education Department may send them a requisition requiring them to fulfil the duty which they have so failed to perform; and if the school board fail within the time limited by such requisition, not being less than three months, to comply therewith to the satisfaction of the Education Department, such board shall be deemed to be a school board in default, and the Education Department may proceed accordingly.

19. Every school board for the purpose of providing sufficient public school accommodation for their district whether in obedience to any requisition or not, may provide, by building or otherwise, schoolhouses properly fitted up, and improve, enlarge, and fit up any schoolhouse provided by them, and supply school apparatus and everything necessary for the efficiency of the schools provided by them, and purchase and take on lease any land, and any right over land, or may exercise any of such powers.

Powers of school board for providing schools.

20. [This section empowered school boards to acquire sites for schools by compulsory purchase, and prescribed regulations governing the procedures to be adopted].

Compulsory purchase of sites. Regulations as to the purchase of land compulsorily.

*   *   *   *   *

23. The managers of any elementary school in the district of a school board may, in manner provided by this Act, make an arrangement with the school board for transferring their school to such school board, and the school board may assent to such arrangement.

Managers may transfer school to school board.

*   *   *   *   *

The Education Department shall consider and have due regard to any objections and representations respecting the proposed transfer which may be made by any person who has contributed to the establishment of such school.

★   ★   ★   ★   ★

Re-transfer of school by school board to managers.

24. Where any school or any interest therein has been transferred by the managers thereof to the school board of any school district in pursuance of this Act, the school board of such district may, by a resolution passed as hereinafter mentioned, and with the consent of the Education Department, re-transfer such school or such interest therein to a body of managers qualified to hold the same under the trusts of the school as they existed before such transfer to the school board, and upon such re-transfer may convey all the interest in the schoolhouse and in any endowment belonging to the school vested in the school board.

A resolution for the purpose of this section may be passed by a majority of not less than two thirds of those members of the school board who are present at a meeting duly convened for the purpose, and vote on the question.

The Education Department shall not give their consent to any such re-transfer unless they are satisfied that any money expended upon such school out of a loan raised by the school board of such district has been or will on the completion of the re-transfer be repaid to the school board.

Every school so re-transferred shall cease to be a school provided by a school board, and shall be held upon the same trusts in which it was held before it was transferred to the school board.

Miscellaneous Powers of School Board

Payment of school fees

25. The school board may, if they think fit, from time to time, for a renewable period not exceeding six months, pay the whole or any part of the school fees payable at any public elementary school by any child resident in their district whose parent is in their opinion unable from poverty to pay the same; but no such payment shall be made or refused on condition of the child attending any public elementary school other than such as may be

selected by the parent; and such payment shall not be deemed to be parochial relief given to such parent.

26. If a school board satisfy the Education Department that, on the ground of the poverty of the inhabitants of any place in their district, it is expedient for the interests of education to provide a school at which no fees shall be required from the scholars, the board may, subject to such rules and conditions as the Education Department may prescribe, provide such school, and may admit scholars to such school without requiring any fee.

Establishment of free school in special cases.

27. A school board shall have the same powers of contributing money in the case of an industrial school as is given to a prison authority by section twelve of "The Industrial Schools Act, 1866;" and upon the election of a school board in a borough the council of that borough shall cease to have power to contribute under that section.

Contribution to industrial schools.

28. A school board may, with the consent of the Education Department, establish, build, and maintain a certified industrial school within the meaning of the Industrial Schools Act, 1866, and shall for that purpose have the same powers as they have for the purpose of providing sufficient school accommodation for their district: Provided that the school board, so far as regards any such industrial school, shall be subject to the jurisdiction of one of Her Majesty's Principal Secretaries of State in the same manner as the managers of any other industrial school are subject, and such school shall be subject to the provisions of the said Act, and not of this Act.

Establishment of industrial school.

Constitution of School Boards

29. The school board shall be elected in manner provided by this Act,—in a borough by the persons whose names are on the burgess roll of such borough for the time being in force, and in a parish not situate in the metropolis by the ratepayers.

School board.

At every such election every voter shall be entitled to a number of votes equal to the number of the members of the school board to be elected, and may give all such votes to one candidate, or may distribute them among the candidates, as he thinks fit.

The school board in the metropolis shall be elected in manner hereinafter provided by this Act.

*   *   *   *   *

Election of school board.

31. With respect to the election under this Act of a school board, except in the metropolis, the following provisions shall have effect:

(1.) The number of members of a school board shall be such number, not less than five nor more than fifteen, as may be determined in the first instance by the Education Department, and afterwards from time to time by a resolution of the school board approved by the Education Department:

*   *   *   *   *

(3.) The Education Department may, at any time after the date at which they are authorised under this Act to cause a school board to be formed, send a requisition to the mayor or other officer or officers who have power to take proceedings for holding the election requiring him or them to take such proceedings, and the mayor or other officer or officers shall comply with such requisition; and in case of default some person appointed by the Education Department may take such proceedings, and shall have for that purpose the same powers as the person in default.

Non-election, &c. of board.

32. If from any cause in any school district the school board either are not elected at the time fixed for the first election, or at any time cease to be in existence, or to be of sufficient number to form a quorum by reason of non-election, resignation, or otherwise, or neglect or refuse to act, the Education Department may proceed in the same manner as if there were a school board acting in such district, and that board were a board in default.

Determination of disputes as to the election of school boards.

33. In case any question arises as to the right of any person to act as a member of a school board under this Act, the Education Department may, if they think fit, inquire into the circumstances of the case, and make such order as they deem just for determining the question,

and such order shall be final unless removed by writ of certiorari during the term next after the making of such order.

*   *   *   *   *

35. A school board may appoint a clerk and a treasurer and other necessary officers, including the teachers required for any school provided by such board, to hold office during the pleasure of the board, and may assign them such salaries or remuneration (if any) as they think fit, and may from time to time remove any of such officers; but no such appointment shall be made, except at the first meeting of such board, unless notice in writing has been sent to every member of the board. Appointment of officers.

*   *   *   *   *

36. Every school board may, if they think fit, appoint an officer or officers to enforce any byelaws under this Act with reference to the attendance of children at school, and to bring children who are liable under the Industrial Schools Act, 1866, to be sent to a certified industrial school before two justices in order to their being so sent, and any expenses incurred under this section may be paid out of the school fund. Officer to enforce attendance at school

School Board in Metropolis

37. The provisions of this Act with respect to the formation and the election of school boards in boroughs and parishes shall not extend to the metropolis; and with respect to a school board in the metropolis the following provisions shall have effect: School board in metropolis

    (1.) The school board shall consist of such number of members elected by the divisions specified in the fifth schedule to this Act as the Education Department may by order fix:

    (2.) The Education Department, as soon as may be after the passing of this Act, shall by order determine the boundaries of the said divisions for the purposes of this Act, and the number of members to be elected by each such division:

    (3.) The provisions of this Act with respect to the constitution of the school board shall extend to the

G

constitution of the school board under this section, and the name of the school board shall be the School Board for London:

(4.) The first election of the school board shall take place on such day, as soon as may be after the passing of this Act, as the Education Department may appoint, and subsequent elections shall take place in the month of November every third year on the day from time to time appointed by the school board:

(5.) At every election for each division every voter shall be entitled to a number of votes equal to the number of the members of the school board to be elected for such division, and may give all such votes to one candidate, or may distribute them among the candidates, as he thinks fit:

(6.) Subject to the provisions contained in this section and in any order made by the Education Department under the power contained in the second schedule to this Act, the members of the board shall, in the city of London, be elected by the same persons and in like manner as common councilmen are elected, and in the other divisions of the metropolis shall be elected by the same persons and in the same manner as vestrymen under The Metropolis Management Act, 1855, and the Acts amending the same;

*   *   *   *   *

(7.) The school board shall proceed at once to supply their district with sufficient public school accommodation, and any requisition sent by the Education Department to such board may relate to any of the divisions mentioned in the fifth schedule to this Act in like manner as if it were a school district, and it shall not be necessary for the Education Department to publish any notices before sending such requisition:

(8.) The Education Department may, in the order fixing the boundaries of such divisions, name some person who shall be the returning officer for the

purposes of the first election of the school board,
and the person who is to be the deputy returning officer in each such division:

(9.) The chairman of the school board shall be elected
by the school board, and any chairman who may
be elected by the board may be elected either
from the members of the board or not, and any
chairman who is not an elected member of the
board shall, by virtue of his office, be a member of the board as if he had been so elected:

(10.) The school board shall apportion the amount required to be raised to meet the deficiency in the
school fund among the different parts of the
metropolis mentioned in the third column of
the first schedule to this Act in proportion to
the rateable value of such parts . . .

          *   *   *   *   *

(11.) For obtaining payment of the amount specified in
any precept sent by the school board to the
rating authority for any part of the metropolis,
the school board, in addition to any other
powers and remedies, shall have the like powers
as the Metropolitan Board of Works have for
obtaining payment of any sum assessed by them
on the same part of the metropolis.

38. The school board for London may pay to the
chairman of such board such salary as they may from
time to time, with the sanction of the Education Department, fix. *Payment of of chairman.*

39. If at any time application is made to the Education Department by the school board for London, or by
any six members of that board, and it is shown to the
satisfaction of the Education Department that the population of any of the divisions mentioned in the fifth
schedule to this Act, as shown by any census taken under
the authority of Parliament, has varied materially from
that shown by the previous census, or that the rateable
value of any of the said divisions has materially varied
from the rateable value of the same division ten years
previously, the Education Department, after such in- *Alteration of number of members*

quiry as they think necessary, may, if they think fit, make an order altering, by way of increase or decrease, the number of members of that and any other division.

United School Districts

Formation by Education Department of united districts.

40. Where the Education Department are of opinion that it would be expedient to form a school district larger than a borough or a parish or any school district formed under this Act, they may, except in the metropolis, by order made after such inquiry and notice as herein-after mentioned, form a united school district by uniting any two or more adjoining school districts, and upon such union cause a school board to be formed for such united school district.

*　*　*　*　*

Contributory Districts

Contributory district.

49. The Education Department may by order direct that one school district shall contribute towards the provision or maintenance of public elementary schools in another school district or districts, and in such case the former (or contributing district) shall pay to the latter (or school owning district or districts) such proportion of the expenses of such provision or maintenance or a sum calculated in such manner as the Education Department may from time to time prescribe.

*　*　*　*　*

Expenses

School fund of school board.

53. The expenses of the school board under this Act shall be paid out of a fund called the school fund. There shall be carried to the school fund all moneys received as fees from scholars, or out of moneys provided by Parliament, or raised by way of loan, or in any manner whatever received by the school board, and any deficiency shall be raised by the school board as provided by this Act.

Deficiency of school fund raised out of rates

54. Any sum required to meet any deficiency in the school fund, whether for satisfying past or future liabilities, shall be paid by the rating authority out of the local rate.

The school board may serve their precept on the rating authority, requiring such authority to pay the amount specified therein to the treasurer of the school board out of the local rate, and such rating authority shall pay the same accordingly, and the receipt of such treasurer shall be a good discharge for the amount so paid, and the same shall be carried to the school fund.

55. In a united district the school board shall apportion the amount required to meet the deficiency in the school fund among the districts constituting such united district in proportion to the rateable value of each such constituent district, and may raise the same by precept sent to the rating authority of each such constituent district.

Apportionment of school fund in united and contributory districts.

Where one school district contributes to the expenses of the schools in another school district the authority of the school owning district may send their precept either to the school board, if any, or to the rating authority of the contributing district, requiring them to pay to their treasurer the amount therein specified, and such authority or board shall pay the same accordingly, and the receipt of the treasurer shall be a good discharge for the same, and such amount, if paid by the school board, shall be paid out of the school fund.

The precept, if sent to the rating authority, either on the default of the school board or otherwise, shall be deemed to be a precept for meeting a deficiency in the school fund, and the provisions of this Act shall apply accordingly.

56. In either of the following cases, that is to say,

(1.) If the rating authority of any place make default in paying the amount specified in any precept of the school board; or

(2.) Where a school board require to raise a sum from any place which is part of a parish,

Remedy of school board on default of rating authority, &c.

then, without prejudice to any other remedy, the school board may appoint an officer or officers to act within such place; and the officer or officers so from time to time appointed shall have within the said place, for the purpose of defraying the sum due from such place, all the powers of the rating authority of levying the local rate and any contributions thereto, and also all the powers of making and levying a rate which he or they would have if the said place were a parish, and such rate were a rate for the relief of the poor, and he or they were duly appointed an overseer or overseers of such parish, and he and they shall have such access to and use of the documents of the rating authority of such place relative to the local rate, and of all the valuation lists and rate books of the parish or parishes comprised in or comprising such place, as he or they may require.

Borrowing by school board.

57. Where a school board incur any expense in providing or enlarging a schoolhouse, they may, with the consent of the Education Department, spread the payment over several years, not exceeding fifty, and may for that purpose borrow money on the security of the school fund and local rate, and may charge that fund and the local rate with the payment of the principal and interest due in respect of the loan.

★   ★   ★   ★   ★

Accounts and Audit

★   ★   ★   ★   ★

Audit of accounts.

60. With respect to the audit of accounts of the school board the following provisions shall have effect:

(1.) The auditor shall be the auditor of accounts relating to the relief of the poor for the audit district in which the school district is situate, or if it is situate in more than one audit district by the auditor of such of the said audit districts as the Poor Law Board may direct . . .

★   ★   ★   ★   ★

(5.) Any ratepayer of the school district may be present at the audit, and may object to the account.

★   ★   ★   ★   ★

Penalty for improper payment of surcharge.

61. Any member or officer of a school board, or manager appointed by them, who authorises or makes, or concurs in authorising or making, any payment or any entry in accounts for the purpose of defraying or making up to himself or any other person the whole or any part of any sum of money unlawfully expended from the school fund, or disallowed or surcharged by any auditor,

shall, on summary conviction, be liable to pay a penalty not exceeding twenty pounds and double the amount of such sum.

★   ★   ★   ★   ★

Defaulting School Board

63. Where the Education Department are, after such inquiry as they think sufficient, satisfied that a school board is in default as mentioned in this Act, they may by order declare such board to be in default, and by the same or any other order appoint any persons, not less than five or more than fifteen, to be members of such school board, and may from time to time remove any member so appointed, and fill up any vacancy in the number of such members, whether caused by removal, resignation, death, or otherwise, and, subject as aforesaid, add to or diminish the number of such members. *(marginal note: Proceedings on default by school board.)*

After the date of the order of appointment the persons (if any) who were previously members of the school board shall be deemed to have vacated their offices as if they were dead, but any such member may be appointed a member by the Education Department. The members so appointed by the Education Department shall be deemed to be members of the school board in the same manner in all respects as if, by election or otherwise, they had duly become members of the school board under the other provisions of this Act, and may perform all the duties and exercise all the powers of the school board under this Act.

The members appointed by the Education Department shall hold office during the pleasure of the Education Department, and when that department consider that the said default has been remedied, and everything necessary for that purpose has been carried into effect, they may, by order, direct that members be elected for the school board in the same manner as in the case of the first formation of the school board. After the date fixed by any such order the members appointed by the Education Department shall cease to be members of the school board, and the members so elected shall be members of the school board in their room, but the members appointed by the Education Department shall not be disqualified from being so elected. Until any such order is made no person shall become a member of the school board otherwise than by the appointment of the Education Department.

Where a school board is not elected at the time fixed for the first election, or has ceased to be in existence, the Education Department may proceed in the same manner as if such board had been elected and were in existence.

*　　*　　*　　*　　*

Expenses incurred on default.

65. The expenses incurred in the performance of their duties by the persons appointed by the Education Department to be members of a school board, including such remuneration (if any) as the Education Department may assign to such persons, shall, together with all expenses incurred by the board, be paid out of the school fund; and any deficiency in the school fund may be raised by the school board as provided by this Act; and where the Education Department have, either before or after the payment of such expenses, certified that any expenses have been incurred by a school board, or any members appointed by them, such expenses shall be deemed to have been so incurred, and to have been properly paid out of the school fund.

Where the members of a school board have been appointed by the Education Department, such school board shall not borrow or charge the school fund with the principal and interest of any loan exceeding such amount as the Education Department certify as mentioned in this Act to be required.

Dissolution of school boards.

66. Where the Education Department are of opinion that in the case of any school district the school board for such district are in default, or are not properly performing their duties under this Act, they may by order direct that the then members of the school board of such district shall vacate their seats, and that the vacancies shall be filled by a new election; and after the date fixed by any such order the then members of such board shall be deemed to have vacated their seats, and a new election shall be held in the same manner, and the Education De-

partment shall take the same proceedings for the purpose of such election as if it were the first election; and all the provisions of this Act relating to such first election shall apply accordingly.

The Education Department shall cause to be laid before both Houses of Parliament in every year a special report stating the cases in which they have made any order under this section during the preceding year, and their reasons for making such order.

Returns and Inquiry

67. On or before the first day of January one thousand eight hundred and seventy-one, or in the case of the metropolis before the expiration of four months from the date of the election of the chairman of the school board, every local authority hereinafter mentioned, and subsequently any such local authority whenever required by the Education Department, but not oftener than once in every year, shall send to the Education Department a return containing such particulars with respect to the elementary schools and children requiring elementary education in their district as the Education Department may from time to time require. *Returns by local authority.*

68. For the purpose of obtaining such returns the Education Department shall draw up forms, and supply to the local authority such number of forms as may be required; and the managers or principal teacher of every school required to be included in any such return shall fill up the form, and return the same to the local authority within the time specified in that behalf in the form. *Mode of obtaining returns.*

69. The returns shall be made in the metropolis by the school board appointed under this Act, in boroughs by the council, and in every parish not situated in a borough or the metropolis by persons appointed for the purpose or by the overseers of such parish. Where a school board is formed under this Act, the returns shall be made by such school board within their district, instead of by the council, persons appointed as aforesaid, or overseers, as the case may be. *Local authority to make returns.*

The persons appointed for the purpose may be appointed as follows; namely, the Education Department may, if they think fit, send to the overseers or other officers who have power to summon a vestry in such parish a requisition to summon, and such overseers or other officers shall summon, a vestry in such parish for the purpose of this section; and such vestry shall appoint two or more persons who shall be the local authority for the purpose of the returns under this Act.

The local authority may, with the sanction of the Education Department, employ persons to assist in making such returns, and may pay those persons such remuneration as the Treasury may sanction. That remuneration, and all such other reasonable expenses incurred by the local authority in making such returns as the Treasury may sanction, shall be paid by the Education Department.

Proceedings on default of authority to make returns.

70. If any local authority fail to make the returns required under this Act, the Education Department may appoint any person or persons to make such returns, and the person or persons so appointed shall for that purpose have the same powers and authorities as the local authority.

Inquiry by inspectors of Education Department

71. The Education Department may appoint any persons to act as inspectors of returns, who shall proceed to inquire into the accuracy and completeness of any one or more returns made in pursuance of this Act, and into the efficiency and suitability of any school mentioned in any such return, or which ought to have been mentioned therein, and to inspect and examine the scholars in every such school. Where there is no return the inspector shall proceed as if there had been a defective return.

Refusal to fill up forms and to admit inspectors.

72. If the managers or teacher of any school refuse or neglect to fill up the form required for the said return, or refuse to allow the inspector to inspect the schoolhouse or examine any scholar, or examine the school books and registers, or make copies or extracts therefrom, such school shall not be taken into consideration among the schools giving efficient elementary education to the district.

Public Inquiry

Public inquiry.

73. Where a public inquiry is held in pursuance of the provisions of this Act the following provisions shall have effect:

(1.) The Education Department shall appoint some person who shall proceed to hold the inquiry:

(2.) The person so appointed shall for that purpose hold a sitting or sittings in some convenient place in the neighbourhood of the school district to which the subject of inquiry relates, and thereat shall hear, receive, and examine any evidence and information offered, and hear and inquire into any subject of the inquiry, with power from time to time to adjourn any sitting.

Notice shall be published in such manner as the Education Department direct of every such sitting (except an adjourned sitting) seven days at least before the holding thereof:

(3.) The person so appointed shall make a report in writing to the Education Department setting forth the result of the inquiry, and stating his opinion on the subject thereof, and his reasons for such opinion, and the objections and representations, if any, made on the inquiry, and his opinion thereon; and the Education Department shall cause a copy of such report to be deposited with the school board (if any), or, if there is none, the town clerk of the borough, or the churchwardens or overseers of the parishes to which the inquiry relates, and notice of such deposit to be published:

(4.) The Education Department may make an order directing that the costs of the proceedings and inquiry shall be paid, according as they think just, either by the district as if they were expenses of a school board, or by the applicants for the inquiry; and such costs may be recovered, in the former case, as a debt due from the school board, or, if there is no school board, as a debt due from the rating authority, and, in the case of the applicants, as a debt due jointly and severally from them; and the Education Department may, if they think fit, before ordering the inquiry to be held, require the applicants to give security for such expenses, and in case of their refusal may refuse to order the inquiry to be held.

Attendance at School

As to
attendance
of children
at school

74. Every school board may from time to time, with the approval of the Education Department, make byelaws for all or any of the following purposes:

(1.) Requiring the parents of children of such age, not less than five years nor more than thirteen years, as may be fixed by the byelaws, to cause such children (unless there is some reasonable excuse) to attend school:

(2.) Determining the time during which children are so to attend school; provided that no such byelaw shall prevent the withdrawal of any child from any religious observance or instruction in religious subjects, or shall require any child to attend school on any day exclusively set apart for religious observance by the religious body to which his parent belongs, or shall be contrary to anything contained in any Act for regulating the education of children employed in labour:

(3.) Providing for the remission or payment of the whole or any part of the fees of any child where the parent satisfies the school board that he is unable from poverty to pay the same:

(4.) Imposing penalties for the breach of any byelaws:

(5.) Revoking or altering any byelaw previously made.

Provided that any byelaw under this section requiring a child between ten and thirteen years of age to attend school shall provide for the total or partial exemption of such child from the obligation to attend school if one of Her Majesty's inspectors certifies that such child has reached a standard of education specified in such byelaw. Any of the following reasons shall be a reasonable excuse; namely,

(1.) That the child is under efficient instruction in some other manner:

(2.) That the child has been prevented from attending

school by sickness or any unavoidable cause:

(3.) That there is no public elementary school open which the child can attend within such distance, not exceeding three miles, measured according to the nearest road from the residence of such child, as the byelaws may prescribe.

The school board, not less than one month before submitting any byelaw under this section for the approval of the Education Department, shall deposit a printed copy of the proposed byelaws at their office for inspection by any ratepayer, and supply a printed copy thereof gratis to any ratepayer, and shall publish a notice of such deposit.

The Education Department before approving of any byelaws shall be satisfied that such deposit has been made and notice published, and shall cause such inquiry to be made in the school district as they think requisite.

Any proceeding to enforce any byelaw may be taken, and any penalty for the breach of any byelaw may be recovered, in a summary manner; but no penalty imposed for the breach of any byelaw shall exceed such amount as with the costs will amount to five shillings for each offence, and such byelaws shall not come into operation until they have been sanctioned by Her Majesty in Council.

It shall be lawful for Her Majesty, by Order in Council, to sanction the said byelaws, and thereupon the same shall have effect as if they were enacted in this Act.

All byelaws sanctioned by Her Majesty in Council under this section shall be set out in an appendix to the annual report of the Education Department.

Miscellaneous

75. Where any school or any endowment of a school was excepted from The Endowed Schools Act, 1869, on the ground that such school was at the commencement of that Act in receipt of an annual parliamentary grant, the governing body (as defined by that Act) of such school or endowment may frame and submit to the Education Department a scheme respecting such school or

Application of small endowments.

endowment.

The Education Department may approve such scheme with or without any modifications as they think fit.

The same powers may be exercised by means of such scheme as may be exercised by means of any scheme under The Endowed Schools Act, 1869; and such scheme, when approved by the Education Department, shall have effect as if it were a scheme made under that Act.

*   *   *   *   *

Inspection of voluntary schools by inspector not one of Her Majesty's inspectors.

76. Where the managers of any public elementary school not provided by a school board desire to have their school inspected or the scholars therein examined, as well in respect of religious as of other subjects, by an inspector other than one of Her Majesty's inspectors, such managers may fix a day or days not exceeding two in any one year for such inspection or examination.

The managers shall, not less than fourteen days before any day so fixed, cause public notice of the day to be given in the school, and notice in writing of such day to be conspicuously affixed in the school.

On any such day any religious observance may be practised, and any instruction in religious subjects given at any time during the meeting of the school, but any scholar who has been withdrawn by his parent from any religious observance or instruction in religious subjects shall not be required to attend the school on any such day.

*   *   *   *   *

Returns by school board.

95. Every school board shall make such report and returns and give such information to the Education Department as the department may from time to time require.

(11) Parliamentary Grant

Parliamentary grant to public elementary school only.

96. After the thirty-first day of March one thousand eight hundred and seventy-one no parliamentary grant shall be made to any elementary school which is not a public elementary school within the meaning of this Act.

No parliamentary grant shall be made in aid of building, enlarging, improving, or fitting up any elementary school. except in pursuance of a memorial duly signed, and containing the information required by the Education Department for enabling them to decide on the application, and sent to the Education Department on or before the thirty-first day of December one thousand eight hundred and seventy.

97. The conditions required to be fulfilled by an elementary school in order to obtain an annual parliamentary grant shall be those contained in the minutes of the Education Department in force for the time being, and shall amongst other matters provide that after the thirty-first day of March one thousand eight hundred and seventy-one— *Conditions of annual parliamentary grant.*

> (1.) Such grant shall not be made in respect of any instruction in religious subjects:
>
> (2.) Such grant shall not for any year exceed the income of the school for that year which was derived from voluntary contributions, and from school fees, and from any sources other than the parliamentary grant;

but such conditions shall not require that the school shall be in connexion with a religious denomination, or that religious instruction shall be given in the school, and shall not give any preference or advantage to any school on the ground that it is or is not provided by a school board:

Provided that where the school board satisfy the Education Department that in any year ending the twenty-ninth of September the sum required for the purpose of the annual expenses of the school board of any district, and actually paid to the treasurer of such board by the rating authority, amounted to a sum which would have been raised by a rate of threepence in the pound on the rateable value of such district, and any such rate would have produced less than twenty pounds, or less than seven shillings and sixpence per child of the number of children in average attendance at the public elementary schools provided by such school board, such school board shall be entitled, in addition to the annual parliamentary grant in aid of the public elementary schools provided by them, to such further sum out of moneys provided by Parliament, as when added to the sum actually so paid by the rating authority, would, as the case may be, make up the sum of twenty pounds, or the sum of seven shillings and sixpence for each such child, but no attendance shall be reckoned for the purpose of calculating such average attendance unless it is an attendance as defined in the said minutes:

Provided that no such minute of the Education Department not in force at the time of the passing of this Act shall be deemed to be in force until it has lain for not less than one month on the table of both Houses of Parliament.

Refusal of grant to unnecessary schools.

98. If the managers of any school which is situate in the district of a school board acting under this Act, and is not previously in receipt of an annual parliamentary grant, whether such managers are a school board or not, apply to the Education Department for a parliamentary grant, the Education Department may, if they think that such school is unnecessary, refuse such application.

The Education Department shall cause to be laid before both Houses of Parliament in every year a special report stating the cases in which they have refused a grant under this section during the preceding year, and their reasons for each such refusal.

Power of schools to take parliamentary grants.

99. The managers of every elementary school shall have power to fulfil the conditions required in pursuance of this Act to be fulfilled in order to obtain a parliamentary grant, notwithstanding any provision contained in any instrument regulating the trusts or management of their school, and to apply such grant accordingly.

Report

Annual report of Education Department

100. The Education Department shall in every year cause to be laid before both Houses of Parliament a report of their proceedings under this Act during the preceding year.

FIRST SCHEDULE

School District	School Board	Local Rate	Rating Authority
The metropolis	The school board appointed under this Act	In the City of London the consolidated rate.	The commissioners of sewers.
		In the parishes mentioned in schedule A and the districts mentioned in schedule B to the Metropolis Management Act, 1855, the general rate and fund raised by the general rate.	In the parishes the vestry, and in the districts the district board.
		In places mentioned in schedule C to the said Act, the rate levied for the purposes of the Metropolitan Poor Act, 1867, and any Act amending the same.	The masters of the bench, treasurer, governors, or other persons who have the chief control or authority in such place
Boroughs, except Oxford	The school board appointed under this Act.	The borough fund or borough rate.	The council
District of the local board of Oxford	The school board appointed under this Act	Rate leviable by the local board.	The local board
Parishes not included in any of the above-mentioned districts.	The school board appointed under this Act.	The poor rate	The overseers

★   ★   ★   ★   ★

SECOND SCHEDULE

FIRST PART

Rules respecting Election and Retirement of Members of a
School Board

1. The election of a school board shall be held at such time, and in such manner, and in accordance with such regulations as the Education Department may from time to time by order pre-

H

scribe, and the Education Department may by order appoint or direct the appointment of any officers requisite for the purpose of such election, and do all other necessary things preliminary or incidental to such election: Provided, that any poll shall be taken in the metropolis in like manner as a poll is taken under "The Metropolis Management Act, 1855," and shall be taken in any other district in like manner as a poll of burgesses or rate-payers (as the case may be) is usually taken in such district.

2. The expenses of the election and taking the poll in any district other than the metropolis shall be paid by the school board out of the school fund.

*   *   *   *   *

10. The first members shall retire from office on the day for retirement which comes next after the expiration of three years from the day fixed for the first election.

11. Members chosen to fill the offices of retiring members shall come into office on the day for retirement, and shall hold office for three years only.

12. Any person who ceases to be a member of the school board shall, unless disqualified as herein-after mentioned, be re-eligible.

*   *   *   *   *

SECOND PART

Rules respecting Resolutions for Application for School Board

1. The meeting of a council for the purpose of passing such a resolution shall be summoned in the manner in which a meeting of the council is ordinarily summoned, and the resolution shall be passed by a majority of the members present and voting on the question.

2. The resolution passed by the persons who would elect the school board shall be passed in like manner as near as may be as that in which a member of the school board is elected, with such necessary modifications as may be contained in any order under the powers of the first part of this schedule, and such powers shall extend to the passing of the resolution in like manner as if it were an election, but the expenses incurred with reference to such a resolution shall be paid by the overseers out of the poor rate.

3. If a resolution is rejected, the resolution shall not be again

proposed until the lapse of twelve months from the date of such rejection.

*   *   *   *   *

THIRD SCHEDULE

Proceedings of School Board

1. The board shall meet for the despatch of business, and shall from time to time make such regulations with respect to the summoning, notice, place, management, and adjournment of such meetings, and generally with respect to the transaction and management of business, including the quorum at meetings of the board, as they think fit, subject to the following conditions:

(a) The first meeting shall be held on the third Thursday after the election of the board, and if not held on that day shall be held on some day to be fixed by the Education Department:

(b) Not less than one ordinary meeting shall be held in each month; one meeting shall be held as soon as possible after every triennial election of members:

(c) An extraordinary meeting may be held at any time on the written requisition of three members of the board addressed to the clerk of the board:

(d) The quorum to be fixed by the board shall consist of not less than three members, and in the case of the metropolis not less than nine members:

(e) Every question shall be decided by a majority of votes of the members present and voting on that question:

(f) The names of the members present, as well as of those voting upon each question, shall be recorded:

(g) No business involving the appointment or dismissal of a teacher, any new expense, or any payment (except the ordinary periodical payments), or any business which under this Act requires the consent of the Education Department, shall be transacted unless notice in writing of such business has been sent to every member of the board seven days at least before the meeting.

*   *   *   *   *

8. Precepts of the board may be in the form given at the end of this schedule.

*   *   *   *   *

Form of Precept

School district of   to wit.

To the council [*or overseers,* &c.] of the borough [*or* parish] of
    . These are to require you, the council [*or* overseers]
of the borough [*or* parish] of   , from and out of
the moneys in the hands of your treasurer [*or* your hands], to pay
on or before the   day of   into the
hands of *A.B.,* treasurer of the school board of the said district,
the sum of   being the amount required for the
expenses of the said school board up to the   of
        18   ; and if there are no moneys in the hands
of your treasurer [*or* your hands] to raise the same by means of
a rate.

(Signed)   C.D.⎱ Members of the school board
              E.F.⎰   of the district of
              G.H. clerk of the said school board

*   *   *   *   *

FIFTH SCHEDULE

DIVISIONS OF METROPOLIS

Name of Division	Name of Division
Marylebone	Westminster
Finsbury	Southwark
Lambeth	City
Tower Hamlets	Chelsea
Hackney	Greenwich

SELECT BIBLIOGRAPHY

(Published in London unless otherwise stated. Standard histories of education are omitted)

A Individual Works

ADAMS, F.
History of the Elementary School Contest in England, 1882
AKENSON, D. H.
The Irish Education Experiment: The National System of Education in the Nineteenth Century, 1970
AMERY, J.
The Life of Joseph Chamberlain, Vol. IV, 1951
ARMSTRONG, R. A.
Henry William Crosskey, his Life and Work, Birmingham, 1895
ARMYTAGE, W. H. G.
A. J. Mundella, 1825-1897, 1951
ARMYTAGE, W. H. G.
The American Influence on English Education, 1967
ARMYTAGE, W. H. G.
'The 1870 Education Act,' *British Journal of Educational Studies*, XVIII, 2, June 1970
BAINES, E.
Education Best Promoted by Perfect Freedom, not by State Endowments, 1854
BAINES, E.
Letters to the Rt. Hon. Lord John Russell on State Education, 1846
BAINES, E.
National Education: Address . . . at Manchester . . . October 11th, 1867, 1867
BAINES, E.
National Education Union: Opening Address at the Educational Conference held at Leeds, December 8th, 1869, 1870
BECK, G. A. (ed).
The English Catholics 1850-1950, 1950

BEST, G. F. A.
'The Religious Difficulties of National Education in England, 1800-1870', *Cambridge Historical Journal*, XII, 2, 1956

BINGHAM, J. H.
The Period of the Sheffield School Board, 1870-1903, Sheffield, 1949

BINNS, H. B.
A Century of Education, Being the Centenary History of the British and Foreign School Society 1808-1908, 1908

BOWEN, D.
The Idea of the Victorian Church, Montreal, 1968

BROUGHAM, H.
A Letter on National Education to the Duke of Bedford, 1839

BROWN, C. K. F.
The Church's Part in Education 1833-1941, with Special Reference to the Work of the National Society, 1942

BURGESS, H. J.
Enterprise in Education, the Story of the Work of the Established Church in the Education of the People prior to 1870, 1958

CHADWICK, O.
The Victorian Church, 1966

CONNELL, W. F.
The Educational Thought & Influence of Matthew Arnold, 1950

COX, J. C. S.
The Life of Cardinal Vaughan, 2 vols, 1910

CRAIK, H.
The State in its Relation to Education, 1884

CRUICKSHANK, M.
Church and State in English Education, 1963

DALE, A. W. W.
The Life of R. W. Dale of Birmingham, 2nd ed, 1899

DALE, R. W.
'Cardinal Manning's Demand on the Rates', *Nineteenth Century*, XIII, January 1883

DALE, R. W.
History of English Congregationalism, 1907

DALE, R. W.
'The Cardinal and the Schools: a Rejoinder', *Nineteenth Century*, XIII, March 1883

DENISON, G. A.
Church Schools and State Interference, A Letter to W. E. Gladstone, 1847
DENISON, G. A.
Notes of my Life, 1805-1878, 1878
DENISON, L. E.
Fifty Years at East Brent, the Letters of George Anthony Denison 1845-1896, 1902
DIAMOND, M. G.
The Work of the Catholic Poor School Committee, 1847-1905 (unpublished M.Ed. thesis, University of Liverpool), 1963
EAGLESHAM, E.
From School Board to Local Authority, 1956
FARRAR, P. N.
'American Influence on the Movement for a National System of Elementary Education in England and Wales, 1830-1870,' *British Journal of Educational Studies,* XIV, 1, November 1965
FITCH, J. G.
'Religion in Primary Schools', *Nineteenth Century* XXXVI, July 1894
GAINE, M.
'The Development of Official Roman Catholic Educational Policy in England and Wales', in *Religious Education,* Darton, 1968
GARVIN, J. L.
The Life of Joseph Chamberlain, 3 vols, 1932-4
GLADSTONE, W. E.
Correspondence on Church and Religion (ed Lathbury, D.C.), 2 vols, 1910
GREGORY, R.
Elementary Education, 1905
GREGORY, R.
'Religion and the Rates' *Nineteenth Century,* XIII, February 1883
HAMILTON, H. H.
The Privy Council and the National Society, 1850
HAMMOND, J. L. and B.,
Lord Shaftesbury, 1939

HODDER, E.
The Life and Work of the Seventh Earl of Shaftesbury, 3 Vols, 1886-7

HOOK, W. F.
On the means of Rendering More Efficient the Education of the People, 1846

HUBBARD, J. G.
The Conscience Clause of the Education Department, 2nd ed, 1865

INGLIS, K. S.
Churches and the Working Classes in Victorian England, 1963

JONES, D. K.
'Lancashire, the American Common School, and the Religious Problem in British Education in the Nineteenth Century', *British Journal of Educational Studies*, XV, 3 October, 1967

KAY-SHUTTLEWORTH, J. P.
Four Periods of Public Education . . . , 1862

KAY-SHUTTLEWORTH, J. P.
Letter to Earl Granville on the Revised Code, 1861

KAY-SHUTTLEWORTH, J. P.
Memorandum on the Present State of the Question of Popular Education, 2nd ed, 1868

KAY-SHUTTLEWORTH, J. P.
Public Education as Affected by the Minutes of the Committee of the Privy Council from 1846-1852, 1853

KEKEWICH, G. W.
The Education Department and After, 1920

KNOX, E. A.
The Tractarian Movement, 1933

McCANN, W. P.
'Trade Unionists, Artisans and the 1870 Education Act', *British Journal of Educational Studies*, XVIII, 2, June 1970

McCLELLAND, V. A.
Cardinal Manning, His Public Life and Influence 1865-1892, 1962

McCLELLAND, V. A.
'The Protestant Alliance and Roman Catholic Schools, 1872-1874', *Victorian Studies*, VIII, 2, December 1964.

MACCOBY, S.
English Radicalism 1786-1832, 1832-52, 1853-86, 1886-1914

MACLURE, E. and ALLEN, W. O. B.
Two Hundred Years: the History of the S.P.C.K. 1698-1898,
1898

MALTBY, S. E.
*Manchester and the Movement for National Elementary
Education*, 1918

MANNING, H. E.
'Is the Education Act of 1870 a Just Law?', *Nineteenth Century*, XII, December 1882

MANNING, H. E.
'Religion and the Rates', *Nineteenth Century*, XIII, February
1883

MATHEWS, H. F.
Methodism and the Education of the People 1791-1851, 1949

MAURICE, F. (ed)
The Life of Frederick Denison Maurice, 2 vols, 1885

MIALL, A.
The Life of Edward Miall, 1884

MIALL, E.
*The Nonconformist's Sketch Book; a Series of Views of a
State-Church and its Attendant Evils*, 1845

MIALL, E.
The Social Influences of the State-Church, 1867

MONTMORENCY, J. E. G. DE.
State Intervention in English Education, 1902

MONTMORENCY, J. E. G. DE.
The Progress of Education in England, 1904

MORLEY, J.
The Life of William Ewart Gladstone, 3 vols, 1903

MORLEY, J.
The Struggle for National Education, 1873

MURPHY, J.
'Church and State in Education: England and Wales', *The
World Year Book of Education, 1966*, 1966

MURPHY, J.
Church, State and Schools in Britain, 1800-1970, 1971

MURPHY, J.
  The Religious Problem in English Education: The Crucial Experiment, 1959
PEEL, A.
  These Hundred Years, A History of the Congregational Union of England and Wales, 1831-1931, 1931
REID, T. W.
  The Life of William Edward Forster, 2 vols, 1888
RICH, E. E.
  The Education Act 1870, 1970
RICHARDS, N. J.
  'Religious Controversy and the School Boards 1870-1902', *British Journal of Educational Studies,* XVIII, 2, June 1970
RIGG, J. H.
  History and Present Position of Primary Education, 1870
RIGG, J. H.
  National Education, 1873
SELBY, D. E.
  'Henry Edward Manning and the Education Bill of 1870', *British Journal of Educational Studies,* XVIII, 2, June 1970
SIMON, B.
  Studies in the History of Education 1780-1870, 1960
SIMON, B.
  Studies in the History of Education: Education and the Labour Movement 1870-1920, 1965
SIMON, B. (ed)
  Education in Leicestershire 1540-1940, 1968
SINCLAIR, J. (ed)
  Correspondence of the National Society with the Lords of the Treasury and with the Committee of Council on Education, 1839
SMITH, F.
  The Life and Work of Sir James Kay-Shuttleworth, 1923
SPALDING, T. A.
  The Work of the London School Board, 2nd ed, 1900
STEPHENS, W. R. W.
  The Life and Letters of Walter Farquhar Hook, 6th ed, 1881
TAYLOR, A. F.
  Birmingham and the Movement for National Education (unpublished Ph.D. thesis, University of Leicester), 1960

TROPP, A.
The School Teachers, 1957
ULLATHORNE, W. B.
Notes on the Education Question, 1857
VAUGHAN, H.
Popular Education in England: the Conscience Clause, the Rating Clause, and the Secular Current, 1868
VIDLER, A. R.
'The Tractarian Movement, Church Revival and Reform', in *Ideas and Beliefs of the Victorians,* 1949
WARDLE, D.
English Popular Education 1780-1970, 1970
WEBB, S.
London Education, 1904

B Reports from Select Committees, Commissions and other Official Sources

(In chronological order)

Reports from the Select Committee appointed to inquire into the present state of the education of the people in England and Wales, and into the application and effects of the grant made in the last session of parliament for the erection of schoolhouses, and the expediency of further grants in aid of education, 1834, 1835

Report from the Select Committee on the education of the poorer classes in England and Wales, 1838

Minutes of the Committee of Council on Education, 1839-58 (continued as *Reports of the Committee of Council on Education,* 1859-1899)

Correspondence between the Committee of Council on Education and the National Society upon the subject of management clauses; copies of the management clauses as amended; and conditions imposed either upon Roman Catholic schools, or schools of Dissenting Bodies, previously to the advance of any sum of money towards the building of such schools, 1849

Report from the Select Committee on education in Manchester and Salford, 1852

Report of the Commissioners appointed to inquire into the state of popular education in England and to consider and report what measures, if any, are required for the extension of sound and cheap elementary education to all classes of people, 1861 (the 'Newcastle Commission')

Correspondence between the Archbishop of Canterbury and Earl Granville, on the subject of the conscience clause, 1866

Return of cases in which, between 1861 and 1867, the Education Department has awarded, or entered into correspondence respecting, grants towards building elementary schools . . . distinguishing cases in which the Department refused a grant on the ground that children of Dissenters might be excluded from such a school, and stating whether the promoters met it by agreeing to insert a conscience clause . . . 1867

Return, confined to the municipal boroughs of Birmingham, Leeds, Liverpool and Manchester, of schools for the poorer classes . . . , by J. G. Fitch and D. R. Fearon, 1870

Return of provisions made by each school board in England and Wales, respecting religious teaching and religious observances by children in board schools, stating the cases in which no such provision is made, 1874-79, etc

Return of the regulations and byelaws at present in force in each school board district in England and Wales respecting the religious teaching . . . , 1888

Reports of the Royal Commission appointed to inquire into the working of the Elementary Education Act, 1886-88 (the 'Cross Commission')

C Other Reports and Pamphlets

British and Foreign School Society: *Annual Reports,* from 1811
Catholic Poor School Committee: *Annual Reports,* 1847-1904
Central Society of Education: *First Publication,* 1837; *Second Publication,* 1838
National Education League: *Report of the First general meeting of the National Education League held at Birmingham . . .*

Oct 1869, 1869 (and subsequent annual reports)

National Education Union: *Authorised Report of the educational conference held at Leeds, Dec. 1869,* 1869 (and subsequent annual reports)

National Society: *Annual Reports,* from 1812

Wesleyan Education Committee: *Annual Reports,* from 1837

INDEX

Allies, T., 77, 78
Anglicans, *see* Church of England
Arnold, M., 53

Baines, E., 18
Baptists, 18
Bentham, J., 10
Birmingham, Education Aid Society, 29, 31, 46; education in, 38; School Board, 71, 72, 74, 77, 78; Town Council, 72, 78
Board schools, *see* School boards
Bright, Jacob, 62, 70
Bright, John, 36, 67
British & Foreign School Society, 12, 22, 60, 63, 81
Bruce, H. A., 28, 44

Cambridge University, 12
Canterbury, Archbishop of, 20, 21, 78
Catholic Poor School Committee, 77, 78
Central Nonconformist Committee, 32, 67
Central Society of Education, 80
Chamberlain, J., 32
Church and state, 11, 12, 13, 14, 15-16, 17, 18ff, 23, 36, 51, 55-7, 111; *see also* Educational finance; individual churches
Church of England, and Committee of Council, 19-21; 'Concordat' of 1840, 20-1, 57; conscience clause, 22-3, 31, 32; lay control of schools, 23-4, 78; parliamentary grant, 80-1; political support, 15, 16, 17; privileged status, 12, 13, 15-16, 17, 26, 31, 36; rate aid, 78; religious instruction, 11, 12, 22-3, 31, 32, 63, 69, 71; school fees, 74; school inspection, 20-1, 26, 57; teacher training, 67; *see also* Church and state; Educational finance; National Society; Tractarians

Church rates, 12, 31
Cobden, R., 27, 59
Committee of Council on Education, 16, 60, 86; and 'Concordat' of 1840, 20-1; conscience clause, 22-3; inspectorate, 20-1, 26; lay control of schools, 23-4; relations with churches, 19-21, 26, 58; teacher training, 21-2, 67 *see also* Education Department, Educational finance
Compulsory attendance, 31, 32, 53-4, 64, 75, 79, 97, 108-9
'Concordat' of 1840, 20-1, 26, 57
Congregationalists, 18, 32
Conscience clause, 22-3, 27, 28, 31, 32, 36, 55, 58, 64, 71, 88, 108
Conservatives, and compulsory attendance, 75; school fees, 73, 75; support for Church of England, 15, 16
'Cowper-Temple clause', 61-2, 64, 70-1, 78, 91
Cross Commission, 70, 77, 78
Crosskey, H. W., 32

Dale, R. W., 32
Denison, G. A., 18-19
Disraeli, B., 63
Dixon, G., 32

Education Department, 25, 70, 78, 86; powers of, 40, 41, 50, 62, 64, 67, 69, 87, 88-91, 92-3, 94-100, 102, 103-15; *see also* Committee of Council on Education
Educational finance, 10, 13, 24-6, 27, 28, 29-30, 43-53, 54, 55, 56, 67, 68, 72-8, 80-1, 83, 86-7, 92, 94, 100-2, 108, 110-12
Educational returns, 88-9, 105-6, 110
'Efficiency', defined, 39
'Elementary education', defined, 37, 86, 87
Endowed Schools Act (1869), 109-10